# Plant and Animal Science Fair Projects

To Patrick, for doing the experiment.

Library of Congress Cataloging-in-Publication Data

Calhoun, Yael.
  Plant and animal science fair projects, revised and expanded using the scientific method / Yael Calhoun.
      p. cm. — (Biology Science Projects Using the Scientific Method)
  Includes bibliographical references and index.
  Summary: "Explains how to use the scientific method to conduct several science experiments about
plants and animals. Includes ideas for science fair projects"—Provided by publisher.
  ISBN 978-0-7660-3421-1
  1. Natural history projects—Juvenile literature. I. Title.
  QH55.C35 2010
  570.78—dc22
                        2009014805

Printed in the United States of America

092009 Lake Book Manufacturing, Inc., Melrose Park, IL

10 9 8 7 6 5 4 3 2 1

**To Our Readers:** We have done our best to make sure all Internet Addresses in this book
were active and appropriate when we went to press. However, the author and the publisher
have no control over and assume no liability for the material available on those Internet sites
or on other Web sites they may link to. Any comments or suggestions can be sent by e-mail
to comments@enslow.com or to the address on the back cover.

♻ Enslow Publishers, Inc. is committed to printing our books on recycled paper. The paper in
every book contains between 10% to 30% post-consumer waste (PCW). The cover board on the
outside of each book contains 100% PCW. Our goal is to do our part to help young people and
the environment too!

Every effort has been made to locate all copyright holders of material used in this book. If any
errors or omissions have occurred, corrections will be made in future editions of this book.

**Illustration Credits:** All illustrations by Tom LaBaff, except California State Polytechnic Unive
Pomona, p. 47 (c); © Corel Corporation, p. 52; Enslow Publishers, Inc., p. 47 (b); University
Lethbridge, p. 47 (a).

**Editorial Revision:** Lily Book Productions

**Design:** Oxygen Design

**Photo Credits:** Shutterstock

**Cover Photos:** Shutterstock

Biology Science Projects
Using the Scientific Method

# Plant and Animal Science Fair Projects

### Revised and Expanded
### Using the Scientific Method

## Yael Calhoun

**Enslow Publishers, Inc.**
40 Industrial Road
Box 398
Berkeley Heights, NJ 07922
USA
http://www.enslow.com

# Contents

Indicates experiments that contain Science Project Ideas.

## INTRODUCTION

# Plant and Animal Experiments and Projects Using the Scientific Method

How do we actually know it takes less energy for some birds to fly hundreds of miles than to stay in one place in the cold? How do we know that some insects live their entire lives in one day, and some trees are over 4,000 years old? How do we know that one, and only one, species of fly can pollinate the cacao flower, the plant from which we get chocolate?

We know these things because scientists have investigated them. As you read this book, your experiments will show how plants and animals behave,

◄ Cacao seeds, imbedded in the fruit of the cacao tree, are used to make chocolate. The cacao's flowers can only be pollinated by a certain species of tiny flies.

 survive, and adapt. Scientists are always learning new information about plants and animals—what they are, what they need to live, and how they affect each other and the planet.

In the 1700s, a Swedish biologist named Carl Linnaeus created a scientific system of naming plants and animals. In Linnaeus' system, each living organism has a name with two parts. The first part is the genus, and the second is the species. For example, the red maple is called *Acer rubrum*.

Identification is the first step to learning about plants and animals, and it is not as easy as you might think. Biologists observe and collect clues about each organism they find. They begin by asking questions.

✓ How does it get its food? Does it make its own, or does it graze or hunt?

✓ What is its body structure? Can it float on water? Does it have a backbone, or is its skeleton on the outside of its body, like a turtle's?

✓ Where does it live? Is it found on the ocean bottom, on a mountaintop, or near a geyser?

After observing and answering specific questions, biologists can decide in which group a living organism should be classified.

As you read this book, your experiments will show how plants and animals have adapted for survival. These adaptations help the organisms get food, survive in different climates, and reproduce. All these things help an organism to be successful. Every species is unique and has its own unique adaptations.

## Experiments and Projects

This book contains lots of fun experiments about plants and animals. You'll also be given suggestions for independent investigations that you can do yourself. Many of the experiments are followed by a section called Science Project Ideas. This section contains great ideas for your own science fair projects.

To do some of the projects in this book, you may need people to help you, because more than one pair of hands may be required. Try to choose helpers who are patient and who enjoy experimenting as much as you do.

The experiments are all easy to do and safe to carry out when the instructions are followed as given. Consult with your school science teacher or some **other responsible adult** to obtain approval before starting any experiments of your own.

If any danger is involved in doing an experiment, it will be made known to you. In some cases, to avoid any danger to you, you'll be asked to work with **an adult**. Please do so. We don't want you to take any chances that could lead to an injury.

Most of the materials you'll need to carry out the projects and experiments described in this book can be found in your home. Several of the experiments may require items that you can buy from a supermarket, a hobby or toy shop, a hardware store, or one of the science supply companies listed in the appendix. As you begin to use this book, show it to one of the science teachers in your school. Perhaps the teacher will allow you and some of your friends to use the school's equipment.

As you do these projects, you will find it useful to record your ideas, notes, data, and anything you can conclude from your experiments in a notebook. That way you can keep track of the information you gather and the conclusions you reach. It will also allow you to refer to other experiments you've done that may be useful to you in later projects.

# How Scientists
# Search for Answers

When scientists have a question to answer, they start by researching. They read scientific literature and consult online science databases that are maintained by universities, research centers, or the government. There, they can study abstracts—summaries of reports—by scientists who have conducted experiments or done similar research in the field.

In this way, they find out whether other scientists have examined the same question or have tried to answer it by doing an experiment. Careful research will tell what kind of experiments, if any, have been done to try to answer the question.

Scientists don't want to repeat experiments that have known and accepted outcomes. Also, they want to avoid repeating any mistakes others may have made while doing similar experiments. If no one else has done scientific work that answers the question, scientists then do further research on how best to do the experiment.

While researching for the experiment, the scientist tries to guess—or predict—the possible results. This prediction is called a hypothesis.

The scientist hopes that a well-researched and carefully planned experiment will prove the hypothesis to be true. At times, however, the results of even the best-planned experiment can be far different from what the scientist expected. Yet even if the results indicate the hypothesis was not true, this does not mean the experiment was a failure. In fact, unexpected results can provide valuable information that leads to a different answer or to another, even better, experiment.

# Using the Scientific Method in Experiments and Projects

## The Scientific Method

A scientific experiment starts when someone wonders what would happen if certain conditions were set up and tested by following a specific process. In other cases, scientists must observe conditions that already exist. For example, in an experiment testing how genetic traits are passed to offspring, we can ask the question: "Do all reptiles have two eyes?" A hypothesis must be a statement because it has to be proved or disproved. Possible hypotheses might be:

✓ All reptiles have two eyes.

✓ Some reptiles may have more than two eyes.

A scientist then designs an experiment or makes observations to collect information to support or to refute the hypothesis. The scientist might observe many species of reptiles and find that one kind of reptile has three eyes. If the scientists's hypothesis was that all reptiles have two eyes, the hypothesis would be proven false. A new question can then be asked. For example, "Why does the tuatara lizard have three eyes?"

When you are doing the experiments in this book, you will need to use a science notebook. Write down your observations, results, and other questions you think of. Write down your conclusions. A science notebook is an important tool for every scientist.

In this book, you will learn techniques scientists use for observing, identifying, and gathering data on plants and animals. You will also learn what plants and animals need to live, how they behave, and what adaptations they have developed. As you learn about plants and animals, you may be amazed and impressed by the incredible diversity of life on our planet.

Scientists may develop logical explanations for the results of their experiments. These explanations, or theories, then must be tested by more experiments. If the resulting data from more experiments provide compelling support for a theory, then that theory could be accepted by the world of science. But scientists are careful about accepting new theories. If the resulting data contradict a theory, then the theory must be discarded, altered, or retested. That is the scientific method.

## Basic Steps in the Scientific Method

The best experiments and science projects usually follow the scientific method's basic steps:

✓ Ask questions about what would happen if certain conditions or events were set up and tested in an experiment.

✓ Do background research to investigate the subject of your questions until you have a main question.

✓ Construct a hypothesis—an answer to your question—that you can then test and investigate with an experiment.

✓ Design and conduct an experiment to test your hypothesis.

✓ Keep records, collecting data, and then analyze what you've recorded.

✓ Draw a conclusion based on the experiment and the data you've recorded.

✓ Write a report about your results.

## Your Hypothesis

Many experiments and science projects begin by asking what conditions made plants or animals the way they are today. In this book's experiment, "Plant Growth Response to Light," the question is: "How does light affect the direction of plant growth?"

How do you search for an answer? For your hypothesis? First, you should observe natural plant growth. How does a plant respond to light? In what direction is the plant growing? Do you notice changes in the plant when weather conditions change?

After your research, you might make an educated guess in answer to the question; this is your hypothesis: "Plants grow in the direction of a light source."

## Designing the Experiment

Your experiment will be structured to investigate whether the hypothesis is true or false. The experiment is intended to test the hypothesis, not necessarily to prove that the hypothesis is right.

The results of a well-designed experiment are more valuable than the results of an experiment that is intentionally designed to give the answer you want. The conditions you set up in your experiment must be a fair test of your hypothesis. For example, in the experiment investigating number of eyes in reptiles you should observe as many species as possible. You can also investigate extinct species of reptiles. You might also look at other species, such as birds, that are related to reptiles. Are there any birds that have more than two eyes? Could that trait have been passed to the bird from an extinct reptile?

**Remember:** To give your experiment or project every chance of success, prepare a hypothesis that is clear and brief. The simpler the better.

By carefully carrying out your experiment you'll discover useful information that can be recorded as data. It's most important that the experiment's procedures and results are as accurate as possible. Design the experiment for observable, measurable results. And keep it simple, because the more complicated your experiment is, the more chance you have for error.

Also, if you have friends helping you with an experiment or project, make sure from the start that they'll take their tasks seriously.

**Remember:** Scientists around the world always use metric measurements in their experiments and projects, and so should you. Use metric liquid and dry measures and a Celsius thermometer.

## Recording Data

Your hypothesis, procedure, data, and conclusions should be recorded immediately as you experiment, but don't keep them on loose scraps of paper. Record your data in a notebook or logbook—one you use just for experiments. Your notebook should be bound so that you have a permanent record. The laboratory notebook is an essential part of all academic and scientific research.

Make sure to include the date, experiment number, and a brief description of how you collected the data. Write clearly. If you have to cross something out, do it with just a single line, then rewrite the correct information.

Repeat your experiment several times to be sure your results are consistent and your data are trustworthy. Don't try to interpret data as you go along. It's better first to record results accurately, then study them later.

You might even find that you want to replace your experiment's original question with a new one. For example, by answering the question, "Can plants get food from water?" you learn that plants need water and nutrient-rich soil to grow. This brings up other questions: "Can plants go for a long period without water? How do desert plants survive with little water and poor soil? Is it possible for there to be too many nutrients in a plant's soil?"

## Writing the Science Fair Report

Communicate the results of your experiment by writing a clear report. Even the most successful experiment loses its value if the scientist cannot clearly tell what happened. Your report should describe how the experiment was designed and conducted and should state its precise results. Following are the parts of a science fair report, in the order they should appear:

### • The Title Page

The title of your experiment should be centered and near the top of the page. Your teacher will tell you what other information is needed, such as your name, grade, and the name of your science teacher.

### • Table of Contents

On the report's second page, list the remaining parts of the report and their page numbers.

### • Abstract

Give a brief overview of your experiment. In just a few sentences, tell the purpose of the experiment, what you did, and what you found out. Always write in plain, clear language.

## • Introduction

State your hypothesis and explain how you came up with it. Discuss your experiment's main question and how your research led to the hypothesis. Tell what you hoped to achieve when you started the experiment.

## • Experiment and Data

This is a detailed step-by-step explanation of how you organized and carried out the experiment. Explain what methods you followed and what materials and equipment you used.

State when the experiment was done (the date, and perhaps the time of day) and under what conditions (in a laboratory, outside on a windy day, in cold or warm weather, etc.). Tell who was involved and what part they played in the experiment.

Include clearly labeled graphs and tables of data from the experiment as well as any photographs or drawings that help illustrate your work. Anyone who reads your report should be able to repeat the experiment just the way you did it. (Repeating an experiment is a good way to test whether the original results were obtained correctly.)

## • Discussion

Explain your results and conclusions, perhaps comparing them with published scientific data you first read about in your research. Consider how the experiment's results relate to your hypothesis. Ask yourself: Do my results support or contradict my hypothesis? Then analyze the answer.

Would you do anything differently if you did this experiment again? State what you've learned as a result of the experiment.

Analyze how your tools and equipment did their tasks and how well you and others used those tools. If you think the experiment could be done better if designed another way or if you've another hypothesis that might be tested, then include this in your discussion.

### • Conclusion

Make a brief summary of your experiment's results. Include only information and data already stated in the report, and be sure not to bring in any new information.

### • Acknowledgments

Give credit to everyone who helped you with the experiment. State the names of these individuals and briefly explain who they are and how they assisted you.

### • References / Bibliography

List any books, magazines, journals, articles, Web sites, scientific databases, and interviews that were important to your research for the experiment.

## Science Fairs

Some of the experiments in this book are followed by a section called Science Project Ideas. These ideas may be appropriate for a science fair. However, judges at science fairs do not reward projects or experiments that are simply copied from a book. For example, a model showing the parts of a plant cell would not impress judges. But data showing how the cell structures of different plants are adapted to changing environmental factors would receive far more consideration.

Science fair judges tend to reward creative thought and imagination. However, it is difficult to be creative or imaginative unless you are really interested in your project, so choose something that appeals to you. Consider, too, your own ability and the cost of materials needed for the project.

If you decide to use a project found in this book for a science fair, you will need to find ways to modify or extend it. This should not be difficult because as you do these projects you will think of new ideas for experiments. It is these new experiments that will make excellent science fair projects because they spring from your own mind and are interesting to you.

If you decide to enter a science fair and have never done so before, you should read some of the books listed in the further reading section. The references that deal specifically with science fairs will provide plenty of helpful hints and lots of useful information that will enable you to avoid the pitfalls that sometimes plague first-time entrants. You will learn how to prepare appealing reports that include charts and graphs, how to set up and display your work, how to present your project, and how to talk to judges and visitors.

Following are some suggestions to consider.

## Some Tips for Success at a Science Fair

Science teachers and science fair judges have many different opinions on what makes a good science fair project or experiment. Here are the most important elements:

**Originality of Concept** is one of the most important things judges consider. Some judges believe that the best science fair projects answer a question that is not found in a science textbook.

**Scientific Content** is another main area of evaluation. How was science applied in the procedure? Are there sufficient data? Did you stick to your intended procedure and keep good records?

**Thoroughness** is next in importance. Was the experiment repeated as often as needed to test your hypothesis? Is your notebook complete, and are the data accurate? Does your research bibliography show you did enough library work?

**Clarity** in how you present your exhibit shows you had a good understanding of the subject you worked on. It's important that your exhibit clearly presents the results of your work.

**Effective Process:** Judges recognize that how skillfully you carry out a science fair project is usually more important than its results. A well-done project gives students the best understanding of what scientists actually do day-to-day.

Other points to consider when preparing for your science fair:

**The Abstract:** Write up a brief explanation of your project and make copies for visitors or judges who want to read it.

**Knowledge:** Be ready to answer questions from visitors and judges confidently. Know what is in your notebook and make some notes on index cards to remind you of important points.

**Practice:** Before the science fair begins, prepare a list of several questions you think you might be asked. Think about the answers and about how your display can help to support them. Have a friend or parent ask you questions and answer them out loud. Knowing your work thoroughly helps you feel more confident when you're asked about it.

**Appearance:** Dress and act in a way that shows you take your project seriously. Visitors and judges should get the impression that you're interested in the project and take pride in answering their questions about it.

**Remember:** Don't block your exhibit. Stand to the side when someone is looking at it.

Projects about plants and animals have special needs with respect to displays. Your observations need to be displayed for the judges. Photograph or draw an example of the species you are investigating. Perhaps you will want to compare an animal's behavior or adaptation to a similar species in another part of the world. Display images of those species and their environments as well. You will certainly have data from your observations. Record your data in a clear and easy to read chart or graph. Be inventive about different ways of showing what you observed.

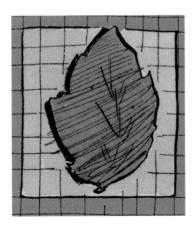

# Safety First

Most of the projects included in this book are perfectly safe, but it's your responsibility to do them only as directed. Some experiments can be dangerous unless certain precautions are taken. The precautions necessary to prevent accidents and to make the experiments safe and enjoyable are easy to follow.

✔ Do any experiments or projects, whether from this book or of your own design, under the supervision of a science teacher or other knowledgeable adult.

✔ Read all instructions carefully before proceeding with a project. If you have questions, check with your supervisor before going any further.

✔ Maintain a serious attitude while conducting experiments. Fooling around can be dangerous to you and to others.

✔ Do not eat or drink while experimenting.

✔ Have a first-aid kit nearby while you are experimenting.

✔The liquid in some thermometers is mercury. It is dangerous to touch mercury or to breathe mercury vapor, and such thermometers have been banned in many states. When doing these experiments, use only non-mercury thermometers, such as those filled with alcohol. If you have a mercury thermometer in the house, **ask an adult** if it can be taken to a local mercury thermometer exchange location.

✔Do not eat or taste solutions unless directed to do so.

And now, on to the experiments!

CHAPTER 1

# CHAPTER 1

# Biological Diversity of Plants and Animals

Would you like to have a plant or animal named after you? Scientists have identified about 1.75 million species, or different types, of living organisms. Most of these are insects. According to some biologists, there may be as many as 100 million living things we still have not found and identified. Every year, new kinds of animals and plants are found. Many species are named after the person who identified them.

One of the many wonders of our planet is that there is such a diversity of living organisms. This incredible array of living things gives the planet something scientists call biodiversity. Biodiversity has three levels:

1. **ecosystems**, or places where organisms live (such as deserts, rain forests, or coral reefs);
2. **species**, or types of organisms (such as saguaro cactus, poison dart frogs, or clown fish); and,
3. **genetics**, or the types of genes, or blueprints, that make up organisms.

◀ Poison dart frogs are a species of frog native to the tropical rain forests of Central and South America.

# EXPERIMENT 1.1

## Eye Location, Prey, and Vision

### Question:

Does the eye location of prey animals increase their range of vision?

### Hypothesis:

Eye location helps grazing animals spot predators.

### Materials:

- a partner
- tape measure
- string or yarn
- scissors
- chalk

### Procedure:

1. Measure and cut a 2.5-meter (8-ft) length of string. Mark a point A on the floor with a piece of chalk. Have a partner hold one end of the string while you hold the other end taut. Tie the piece of chalk to the end of the string and draw a 2.5-meter (8-ft) arc (semicircle) around point A (see Figure 1a).

# Figure 1.

a)

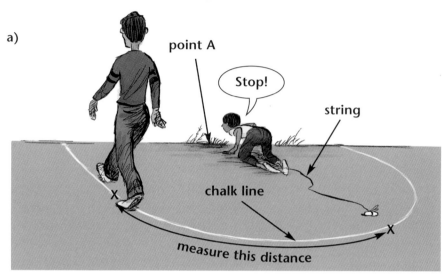

b)

a) Holding a piece of chalk tied to a 2.5-meter (8-ft) piece of string, draw an arc around the person at point A. As the predator, slowly walk around to the left along the arc.

b) When the grazer turns her head 8 centimeters (3 in) to the left, does it change her field of view?

2. Have your partner, still at point A, get down on her hands and knees. She will put her head down and pretend she is eating something on the ground without turning her head to either side. You can be a predator and stand directly 2.5 meters (8 ft) behind her. Slowly walk to her left along the arc marked in chalk. Your partner will say "stop" when she sees you, the predator, in her field of vision. Mark this spot.

3. Cover the arc with a piece of string to show the distance from your starting point to when you were spotted. Then measure the length of the string to determine how far you traveled before being spotted. Repeat the experiment three times and record the results.

4. Find the average spotting distance for your partner's eyes (which represent the eyes as they are set in a predator) by adding the three distances together and dividing by three.

5. Now repeat the steps, but have your partner turn her head 8 centimeters (3 in) to the left side so that her left eye now sees what a grazing animal (with eyes set wider apart on it skull) would see. Then begin moving to the left along the arc (see Figure 1b). Repeat this three times and record the results.

6. Find the average spotting distance for the prey's eyes by adding the three distances together and dividing by three.

7. Graph your data (see Figure 2). Which eye location affords the most protection (time to see the danger) while grazing? Would grazing animals with eyes set close together have an advantage or disadvantage while grazing?

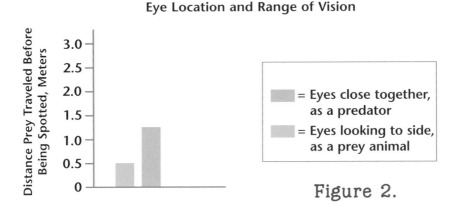

Figure 2.

You can make a bar graph to show the relationship between type of animal (predator or prey) and its field of vision.

# Results and Conclusions

Over the past 3.8 billion years, life has become amazingly diverse. But, even with all this diversity, when it comes to eating, there are still only a few categories into which all animals fall. The two major categories are those that eat other animals and those that eat plants.

Predators are the animals that hunt other animals. They need to sense depth and exact location in order to capture their prey. To do this, predators, including eagles, lions, humans, and wolves, have evolved binocular (using two eyes) vision. Their eyes are set in their heads in such a way that what one eye sees overlaps with what the other eye sees. This binocular vision creates a three-dimensional image.

On the other hand, grazing animals, such as rabbits and deer, do not have to catch their food. But they do need to spot predators. Grazing animals have eyes that are set apart, which gives them a wide field of vision, especially while grazing.

What are the advantages and disadvantages of having such wide-set eyes? Would grazing in a herd, as deer and zebras do, give the individual more protection? How would a lack of binocular vision, or less acute vision, affect a predator trying to hunt an animal on the move?

Observe (or look at pictures of) cats, dogs, rabbits, owls, deer, and cows. Based on the way their eyes are set in their skulls, do you think they are predators or prey? Do some research about what these animals eat to see if you are correct.

 ## Science Project Ideas

- Research the different types of body structures found in animals (for example, find out the definitions and some examples of bilateral and radial symmetry; the definitions and some examples of endoskeletons and exoskeletons). What other body types can you identify? How are they adapted to living in particular habitats?

- There are many different types of animal eyes. Do some research and make a chart of what you learn. Find out what sea creature has between 50 and 100 eyes and how our eyes differ from those of a butterfly or a dog. What prey animal has binocular vision so that it can jump from branch to branch in trees? Why do cats' eyes reflect at night?

# EXPERIMENT 1.2

## Plants, Animals, and Their Niches

### Question:
How many niches can you find?

### Hypothesis:
In any given study site, different niches can be found.

### Materials:
- plant, animal, and insect field guides (check the library)
- large empty can
- tape measure
- 2 study sites
- binoculars (optional)
- magnifying glass (optional)

If the planet Earth consisted only of flat fields of grass and warm freshwater lakes, do you think there would be as many different species of plants and animals? We know that our planet has dark ocean floors, caves without light, scorching deserts, hot springs, rocky mountaintops, marshes, and bogs. And life has found its way into all of these very different places.

During the 3.8 billion years that life has been evolving on the planet, organisms have adapted (changed in order to fit) to all its nooks and crannies. The term *niche* is used to describe the specific place a species occupies. A niche is more than just a general area or habitat, such as an ocean, a desert, or an oak forest. A niche includes the specific place in which an organism lives and reproduces. It also includes the available resources and how an organism obtains and supplies those resources. Resources are such things as food, water, and materials to make homes.

For example, as ecologist Eugene Odum said, "The ecological niche of an organism depends not only on where it lives but also on what it does. By analogy, it may be said that the habitat is the organism's 'address,' and the niche is its 'profession,' biologically speaking."

# Procedure:

1. Remember that an important part of biological science is observation and classification. Choose two study sites to compare: The sites could be one sunny side and one shady side near your house; a dead tree and a living tree; or the topsoil in a field and a wetland edge. Many biologists also consider vertical changes when looking at niches. For example, they would look at the different organisms found from the sediment on the bottom of a pond to the surface of the water; or from the fallen leaves rotting at the bottom of a tree to the canopy (top branches and leaves).

2. After you choose your two study sites, record the following information for each site. If, for example, you are using an oak tree, record the information for fallen leaves at the base of the tree (site #1) and for the tree canopy (site #2). Be sure to measure the size of your study site. Both sites should be about the same size. Use field guides to identify species that are not familiar to you.

✓ **Animal activity.** Observe the site for at least 15 minutes in the morning, noontime, and evening (if possible) for several days. List the type of animal species you see and the number of each. For example: black-capped chickadees (7); spiders (2); red squirrels (4).

✓ **Animal signs.** Record such signs as scat (feces), tracks, eaten pinecones, and nests.

✓ **Insects and invertebrates.** Dig a hole and place an empty can flush with the ground surface. After a day, carefully remove the animals that you find in the can, identify and record the total number of different species found, and carefully return the creatures to their home. Do this for several days.

✓ **Plants.** Identify as many plants as possible. Make a chart of location (growing on the tree, under the tree, at the pond edge). Record any animal life found on the plants.

✓ **General site observations.** For example: "The place is hot and dry most of the time. It is busy with animals during the early morning; quiet at noon."

3. Analyze your findings. How many species were found in each niche? Which niche has the greater diversity (different kinds) of life? The higher total number of individual organisms? Why do you think this might be so?

# Results and Conclusions

Organisms have adapted to thrive in a variety of different niches. Think about what organisms need to survive. Do you think the organisms you found in the first site are adapted to living in the second? Do you think some organisms have adapted to live in more areas, or niches, than others?

Science Project Ideas

- Some creatures have evolved to live in the dark. Find out about life in the Movile Cave in Romania, a recently discovered cave that has existed in darkness for over 5.5 million years. Scientists found forty-eight species of animals living there, and thirty-one were new discoveries. What adaptations have allowed the organisms to survive? What other species living in darkness have been identified?

- Find out about ecotourism in rain forests around the world and in old growth forests in the northwestern United States. Find out how some people and organizations are working to preserve habitats by helping people earn a living from the land without destroying it. How does ecotourism help organisms with very specific niches to survive? What else can be done to help?

# EXPERIMENT 1.3

## Animals and Seed Dispersal

### Question:

Do animals help plants spread their seeds?

### Hypothesis:

Seeds can attach to an animal's skin or fur, moving them to different places.

### Materials:

- long pants
- safety pins
- piece of fake fur or felt
- field guides for plants, trees, shrubs, grasses, or flowers (check your library)
- field and forest
- magnifying glass (optional)
- glue
- plastic wrap
- Velcro strip
- paper

# Procedure:

1. Use safety pins to attach a piece of fake fur or felt to your pant leg, from the knee to the ankle (see Figure 3).

2. Take a walk through the woods or a field. After your walk, remove any seeds from each pant leg. Glue one of each type of seed you collected from each leg to a chart, and record the numbers of each.

3. Identify the seeds (grasses, burrs, etc.). How would you, an animal, have increased some plants' chances of survival (meaning, the chances of the species to reproduce)? Which leg provided the better surface for transport? How could you present your results in a graph?

4. If one pant leg (or shoe) were covered in wet mud, would more seeds stick? Would a smooth-surfaced animal (such as a salamander) spread as many seeds as, say, a rabbit? Try different surfaces, such as plastic wrap or Velcro. How many ways can you list that animals help to spread seeds?

5. Find out about squirrels and red cedar seeds. What might a bird with muddy feet carry to an island? How do islands or areas after a volcanic eruption get vegetated? (Research, for example, the plants on Mount Saint Helens.)

## Figure 3.

Attach a piece of fake fur or felt to the bottom half of one pant leg. What sticks to your "fur"? What sticks to the other leg?

# Results and Conclusions

Basic needs are what you need to stay alive, such as food, water, and protection from the weather and predators. Think about how much energy you would use if you, alone, had to provide these necessities. This is one reason people work together—it saves energy, which increases the chances of survival. For the same reasons, animals and plants have evolved in ways that enable them to work together. And, just as there are many kinds of organisms on the planet, there are many ways they use each other for survival.

This is not to say that plants and animals make a conscious decision to help each other, as people in a community do. It means that over time, for whatever reason, organisms evolved in ways that work to benefit themselves and maybe each other. When an organism depends on another type of organism for survival, it is called symbiosis. There are several types.

✓ **Parasitism.** In parasitism, one creature lives in or feeds from another one. An example is a tick or a tapeworm feeding on a moose. The host (the moose) may be weakened, but it does not necessarily die from the infestation.

✓ **Commensalism.** In commensalism, one species benefits but the other is not affected. An example is an orchid growing on a tree for support and exposure to the light. The orchid does not harm the tree.

✓ **Mutualism.** Both organisms benefit from a mutually symbiotic relationship. An example is the oxpecker, a bird that sits on a zebra's back and eats ticks. The animals benefit in more ways than one. Not only is the bird fed and the zebra tick-free, but also the bird flies off when there is danger, which alerts the zebra to the danger. Perhaps the most common example of mutualism is between insects and flowers. Insects are attracted to the food in the flowers. While eating the nectar, the insects get covered in pollen. On the visit to the next flower, pollen drops off and fertilizes it. In this way, plants reproduce.

One way that animals help plants to survive as a species is by spreading their seeds. When seeds can land in different areas, it increases the plant's chances of survival. Some animals eat the fruit of a plant, then move on and deposit the seeds in their feces. Other animals simply transport seeds on their feet or fur. Why is it helpful to the survival of a plant if its seeds get spread to other areas?

Science Project Idea

- Plants and animals help each other survive in other ways too. Insects use plants for food, homes, and nesting sites. Find a stand of plants and examine the leaves for red or brown bumps. These are insect galls, or eggs. Observe the plants for 15 minutes in the morning, at noon, and in the evening for several days. Record the incidence of insect activity (bees, ants, butterflies, beetles, aphids) on the plants. You can also do this observation for a stand of trees and record the incidence of all animal visitation (deer, squirrel, insects, birds). Is there a period of the day when animal activity is greater? Is there a tree or a habitat (marsh, edge between a field and a forest, lakeshore) that has more activity than another? Why might this be?

# EXPERIMENT 1.4

## Identifying Plant Cells

### Question:

Can you identify different plant cells?

### Hypothesis:

Plant cells have a unique structure that can be used in identification.

### Materials:

- prepared slides of various parts of plants (from a science supply company or your science teacher)—root cross section: e.g., buttercup (*Ranunculus*); leaf cross section: e.g. lilac (*Syringa*); stem cross section: e.g., corn (*Zea mays*)
- compound microscope with light source
- botany book

The smallest unit of life is a cell. Most cells can be seen only through a microscope. Cells are the basic building blocks of all living things. Plants have specialized cells to do different jobs. Each specialized cell contains different structures to do its job.

A plant root has an outside layer called the epidermis. It is made up of loosely packed cells that allow water to pass through easily. Roots also have structures called vascular bundles that contain xylem and phloem cells. These are the tubes that transport water, minerals, and food throughout the plant. The cortex surrounds these bundles. The inner-most layer of the cortex is called the endodermis and is arranged in a ring around the vascular bundles (see Figure 4a).

A waxy leaf has an outside layer called the cuticle. This prevents the leaf from drying out. Openings on the underside of the leaf are called stomata. They allow water and gases to pass through. Guard cells on either side of each stoma open and close it. The mesophyll layer of cells are involved in photosynthesis (see Figure 4b). A plant stem has a cortex, an epidermis, and vascular bundles with the xylem and phloem cells (see Figure 4c).

Part of being a biologist is learning to recognize and to identify differences in cells of organisms.

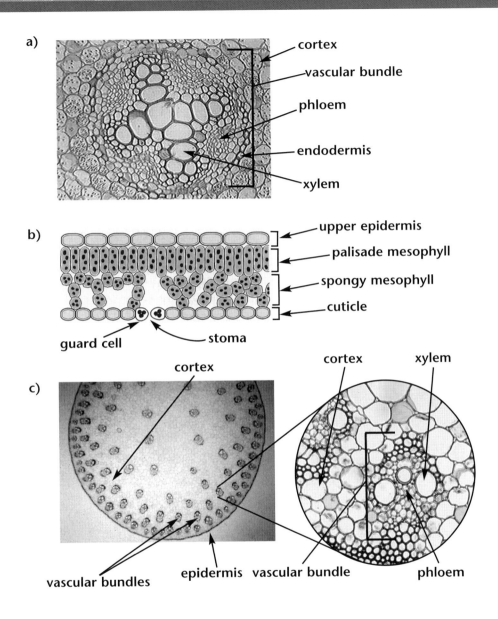

a) cortex
vascular bundle
phloem
endodermis
xylem

b) upper epidermis
palisade mesophyll
spongy mesophyll
cuticle
guard cell
stoma

c) cortex
cortex    xylem
vascular bundles
epidermis  vascular bundle
phloem

## Figure 4.

a) A slide of root cells of a buttercup plant (*Ranunculus*) shows a ring of vascular bundles that contain xylem and phloem cells.

b) The cross section of a lilac leaf (*Syringa*) shows the epidermis, cuticle, and guard cells.

c) A cross section of a corn (*Zea mays*) stem shows the epidermis, cortex, and vascular bundles with xylem and phloem cells.

## Procedure:

1. Using a compound microscope with light source, view prepared slides of various plant parts. Look at the slides under low power and high power. If you need help using a microscope, ask your science teacher or another knowledgeable adult to help you.

2. In your science notebook, draw what you see on the slide and label the different parts of the plant cell. For the root cells, label the epidermis; the vascular bundle, which is made up of the phloem and xylem; the cortex; and the endodermis, which is the ring of cells around the vascular bundle (see Figure 4a). For the leaf cells, label the cuticle, the upper epidermis, a guard cell, a stoma, the palisade mesophyll, and the spongy mesophyll (see Figure 4b). For the stem cells, label the epidermis, the cortex, and the vascular bundles, which include the xylem and the phloem vessels (see Figure 4c). Notice that in the corn, the vascular bundles are scattered.

## Results and Conclusions

Plants have been able to adapt to the many different environmental conditions on the planet because they have many different types of cells. How do root cells differ from the cells found in a leaf? Think about the relationship between structure (how something is made) and function (the job it does). Why would loosely packed cells in plant roots help the plant absorb water? Why would the waxy coating on certain leaf cells have a different function? Make a chart and identify other cell differences and explain how the structure of a cell relates to its function.

# Science Project Ideas

- Flowering plants are divided into two classes—monocots and dicots. Grasses, corn, sugarcane, lilies, and wheat are examples of monocots. Peas, lilacs, roses, alfalfa, and beans are some dicots. Compare the root, stem, and leaf cross sections of a dicot and a monocot. Are the cells different, or is the organization of the cells different?

- Compare a leaf cross section of a succulent plant, such as agave, with that of an aquatic plant, such as elodea. Where are the stomata on the succulent plant? What are the differences in the epidermal, or outer, layers? Find rooted plants growing at the edge of a pond. Compare its stem (**have an adult** help you cut a cross section) with a land plant's stem cross section. Why would a plant with roots in the water need a spongy center? (Think about transport of gases to the roots.)

# EXPERIMENT 1.5

## Identifying Muscle Cells

### Question:

Can you identify different muscle cells?

### Hypothesis:

Muscle cells vary based on their function.

### Materials:

- prepared slides of human skeletal, smooth, and cardiac muscle (from a science supply company or your science teacher)
- compound microscope with light source
- human physiology book

There are three kinds of muscle cells in the human body: skeletal muscle cells, cardiac muscle cells, and smooth muscle cells. Skeletal muscle cells work together to move the bones. They are among the largest cells in the body. For example, the muscle cells in the thigh may be as long as 35 centimeters (14 in). These cells are often called muscle fibers because of their length. A person can control skeletal muscle cells voluntarily. Skeletal muscle is composed of bundles of cylinder-shaped cells arranged in a regular, striped pattern. Unlike the other types of muscle cells, each skeletal muscle cell has many nuclei (the part of the cell that contains the genetic information).

Cardiac muscles are found only in the heart. They allow the heart to pump blood throughout the body. Cardiac muscles start their own contraction—a person does not have to think about them. Special structures called intercalated discs, located between these cells, allow the signals to move from one cell to another so that the heart beats in a rhythm. Cardiac muscles are cylinder-shaped and arranged in a branching pattern. Each cardiac muscle cell has one nucleus.

Smooth muscles are the muscles that line the hollow organs in the body, including the stomach, the blood vessels, and the intestines. They produce long, slow contractions that a person usually does not control by thinking. A smooth muscle cell is shaped like a long, thin spindle and has one nucleus.

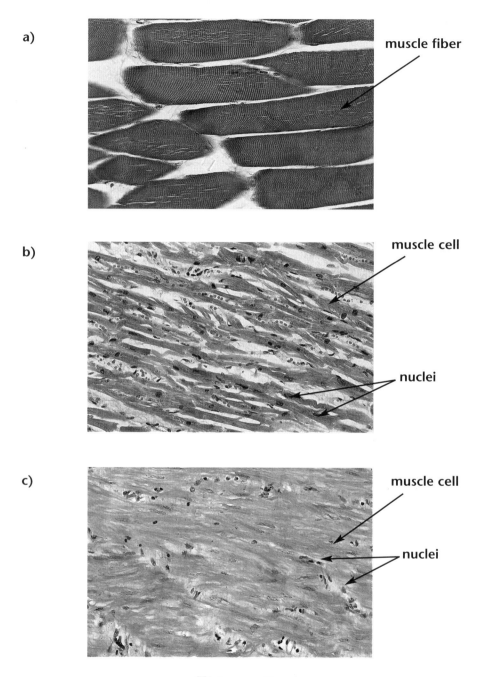

## Figure 5.

a) A slide of skeletal muscle shows muscle cells (fibers).
b) A slide of cardiac muscle shows muscle cells and nuclei.
c) A slide of smooth muscle shows muscle cells and nuclei.

# Procedure:

1. Using a compound microscope with light source, view prepared slides of human smooth, skeletal, and cardiac muscle cells at magnifications of 40X and 100X.

2. Draw what you see and label your cell drawings in a science notebook. For skeletal muscle, label the muscle fiber (see Figure 5a). For the cardiac muscle, label the muscle cell and the nucleus (see Figure 5b). For the smooth muscle, label the muscle cell and the nucleus (see Figure 5c).

3. Read about the three types of muscles in a human physiology book. Why do you think the skeletal muscle fibers are rounder and larger than the smooth muscle cells? Think about where these muscles are found and what function they serve. Why does a cardiac muscle cell have a very different structure than other types of muscle cells? Why is this structure necessary to the proper functioning of the heart?

## Results and Conclusions

Your body contains many different kinds of cells. Each cell type has a different structure because it does a different job. The different types of muscle cells have different structures because they have different functions in the body.

## Science Project Ideas

- Study slides of various plant and animal cells. How do plant cells differ from animal cells? Draw and label pictures of several different plant and animal cells. Describe the differences and how structure affects function.

- Sometimes animals or plants are only one cell. **With an adult**, investigate a pond or a lake and see what kinds of single-celled organisms you can identify. Compare what you find a) near the edges that are without plants; b) among the plants growing along the edges; and, c) in the pond center (if **an adult** can take you there).

# EXPERIMENT 1.6

## Land Plants and Aquatic Plants

### Question:
How do land and aquatic plants differ?

### Hypothesis:
Land and aquatic plants have adaptations that are suited to their different habitats.

### Materials:
- **an adult**
- 6 one-liter plastic bottles
- ruler
- permanent marker
- 3 aquatic plants (use a handful of duckweed or pondweed, or buy 3 similar aquatic plants at an aquarium supply store)
- water (pond water if possible)
- 3 similar house or garden plants
- strong scissors
- potting soil
- scale
- aluminum foil
- oven
- oven mitts
- sunlight

# Procedure:

1. With strong scissors, cut the tops from six one-liter plastic bottles so that each bottle is 18 centimeters (7 in) tall. With a permanent marker, label three of the bottles A-1, A-2, and A-3. Fill the three bottles with water and mark the water level with the marker.

2. Add one similar aquatic plant to each bottle (see Figure 6). Label the other three bottles L-1, L-2, and L-3 and fill them with potting soil. Plant three similar land plants in the soil.

3. Place all six containers in a sunlit area. Add water to the A bottles as needed to keep the water level at the line you marked. Water the L plants when the top centimeter of soil is dry. If the plants do not appear healthy after three days, start over with new plants. Allow the plants to grow for one more week after they have been growing well for three days.

4. Carefully remove the plants in A-1, A-2, L-1, and L-2 from their containers. Save the plants in A-3 and L-3 for your science fair presentation. Gently wash the soil from the roots of L-1 and L-2.

5. Look at all four plants and estimate what percentage of the plant is made up of roots.

   What are the leaf characteristics—waxy, thin, dark? Do the leaves have a good ability to retain water? Determine this by putting one leaf from each plant in the sun and recording how long it takes to shrivel. What are the plant similarities?

6. What percentage of each plant is water? To determine this, pat one aquatic plant dry and weigh it. Record this weight in your notebook. Also weigh one land plant and record this weight. **Have an adult** place the different types of plants on separate pieces of aluminum foil and

bake them in an oven at 121°C (250°F) for about an hour or until the leaves are crumbly. **The adult** should use oven mitts to remove them. Once they have cooled, reweigh them. This is the dry weight. Subtract the dry weight from the wet weight. The difference is the weight of water that was in the plant. To find the percentage of water in each plant, divide the difference between its wet and dry weights by its wet weight and multiply by 100.

$$\frac{(\text{wet weight} - \text{dry weight})}{\text{wet weight}} \times 100 = \%\ \text{water}$$

In what ways do land and aquatic plants differ? How do your observations demonstrate the changes in structure and function that plants had to develop to live on land?

## Figure 6.

You can study land and aquatic plants. In three of the bottles, place pond water with an aquatic plant. In the other three bottles, place land plants in potting soil.

# Results and Conclusions

Over millions of years, some plants have adapted from growing in water to growing on land. They evolved specialized cell types. Changes in the plant's cell structure have allowed plants to get water, sunlight, and nutrients in new land habitats. Following are some specialized structures that allow plants to live on land:

- ✓ Roots can store nutrients and water from the soil.

- ✓ Waxy leaves and thick stems prevent land plants from drying out in the air.

- ✓ Stomata—openings in the leaves—open and close to allow the exchange of gases while preventing water from escaping.

- ✓ Vessels carry water and minerals between the leaves and the roots.

- ✓ Pollen or seeds help plants reproduce without being in the water.

- ✓ Lignins, substances that make the plants stiff, support the plants in the air.

Science Project Ideas

- Use a compound microscope, with light source, to

  a) compare the stem cross sections of both types of plants by looking for xylem and phloem tubes; and

  b) compare the leaf structure by looking for stomata. Are these plants adapted to survive in the other's conditions? To find out, plant the aquatic plants in soil, and the land plants in water.

- Investigate human uses for plants, both current and old. Make a chart, including pressed plants when available. (Do not pick an unidentified plant because it may be poisonous or endangered.) What plants do animals use for food and for homes?

# CHAPTER 2

# Plant and Animal Survival Needs

Have you ever gone running and thought, "I just don't have the energy to make it to the finish"? Energy is the capacity to do work. Living organisms need energy to do everything—to live, to grow, to reproduce, and even to think. All the chemical reactions needed for these life processes are called metabolism.

Metabolism is a process performed in cells to acquire and use nutrients and energy from the environment. It is the same process for plants and animals. The process used to keep your brain cells alive is the same process used by a plant to keep its cells alive (glycolysis). The difference is that plants get their energy directly

◄ All living things need energy to survive. Plants get their energy from sunlight during photosynthesis.

from the sun to make food (photosynthesis), while animals must get their energy from those plants or from animals that have eaten those plants.

The major energy source on our planet is the electromagnetic energy from the sun. Plants absorb the sun's energy to make food (carbohydrates, or sugar). When you see a cat or a lizard basking in the sun, it is only to get warm. The only way an animal can get the energy it needs to live is by eating a plant or another animal. The sun's energy links living things together in what is called a food web or a food chain.

# EXPERIMENT 2.1

## Plant Growth and Light

### Question:
How does light affect plant growth?

### Hypothesis:
Light is necessary for plants to grow.

### Materials:
- 36 pinto beans or sunflower seeds
- water
- bowl
- scale
- 12 paper cups
- potting soil
- scissors
- saucers (or plastic lids for under the cups)
- sunlight
- permanent marker
- ruler
- graph paper
- paper towel

### Procedure:

1. Soak 36 pinto beans or sunflower seeds in water overnight to soften the seed coats.

2. With scissors, carefully poke three small holes for water drainage in the bottom of 12 paper cups. With a permanent marker, label 4 cups FULL LIGHT—FL, 4 cups PARTIAL LIGHT—PL, and 4 cups DARK—D (see Figure 7). Fill each cup with potting soil and place them on saucers.

3. Plant 3 seeds in each cup of soil, and water each cup. Keep all the cups in the same place until the seeds germinate (sprout). Choose one seedling in each pot that has the strongest stem and the most leaves. Remove the other seedlings.

**Figure 7.**

To find out how sunlight affects plant growth, place the light group in full sunlight. Place the partial-light group in sunlight during part of the day and in a dark closet for the remainder of the time. Place the dark group in a dark, warm closet or cupboard.

4. Place the 4 full-light cups in a sunny window, and the 4 dark cups in a dark, but not cold, cupboard or closet. Place the partial-light cups in the light for half of the daylight time (perhaps while you are at school), then with the dark plants the rest of the daylight time. Water the plants as needed (when the top 2 centimeters (0.8 in) of soil gets dry).

5. After two weeks, measure the height of each plant and record the plant growth in all the pots. Record the following data for the pots in each group:

   a. **Average plant height.** Measure the plant height from the soil surface to the top of the plant.

   b. **Average number of leaves.** Count the total number of leaves on all plants in the group, and divide by the number of plants in the group.

   c. **Average leaf size.** Choose a leaf that is the size of most of the other leaves. Place the leaf on a piece of graph paper. Draw a square around the leaf and measure the area of the square. Trace the leaf inside the square and count the number of graphing squares the leaf covers (see Figure 8). Suppose the box is 16 cm² and has 64 squares. If the leaf covers 18 squares, then the leaf size is

$$\frac{64 \text{ squares}}{16 \text{ cm}^2} = \frac{18 \text{ squares}}{x \text{ cm}^2}$$

   When you solve for x, your answer is 4.5. The leaf is 4.5 cm².

   d. **Color of the leaves.**

   e. **Average wet weight.** Use three plants from each group. (Save the fourth pot from each group for your project presentation.) Wash the soil from the roots and pat the plants dry with a paper towel. Weigh the plants. (It is called wet weight because the plant has water inside it). To obtain the average wet weight of each group, weigh the group together and divide by the number of plants in the group.

6. Graph your results for the following: the average number of leaves; the average leaf size; and the average wet weight. What were the differences in growing conditions? Which plants produced the most biomass (material made from growing organisms)?

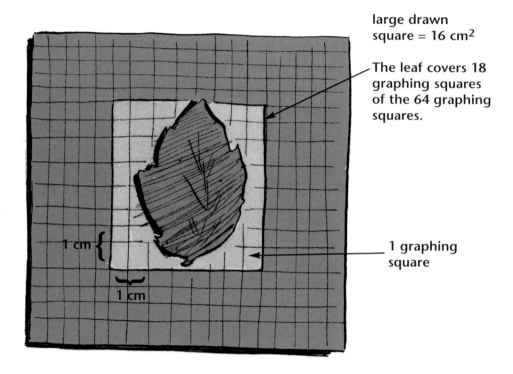

large drawn
square = 16 cm$^2$

The leaf covers 18 graphing squares of the 64 graphing squares.

1 cm

1 cm

1 graphing square

## Figure 8.

Place one leaf on a piece of graph paper. Draw a square around the leaf. Trace the leaf inside the square. By determining the number of squares that the leaf covers, you can calculate the area of the leaf.

# Results and Conclusions

Plants absorb energy from the sun to make their own food. The energy from the sun allows plants to change water and carbon dioxide into sugar (carbohydrates). The process is called photosynthesis:

**carbon dioxide + water + light energy (sunlight)** $\longrightarrow$ **sugar + oxygen.**

The plants then use or store these sugars.

Sunlight provides animals with energy as well. But its effect is indirect. The only way for animals to tap into this energy is to eat the plants, or to eat animals that eat the plants. In this way, most animals also need sunlight to live.

 Science Project Idea

- You can expand on Experiment 2.1 by answering questions such as the following: Does the time of day the plants receive light or the direction the window faces make a difference? If you vary the air temperature or amount of water, does that compensate for the lack of light? What other conditions could you change? (Think about blocking some light to certain leaves and not others.) Do the results change if you run the experiment over a longer period of time?

# EXPERIMENT 2.2

## Plant Growth and Different Types of Light

### Question:

How do different types of light affect plant growth?

### Hypothesis:

Plants do not use all light colors (wavelengths) equally.

### Materials:

- **an adult**
- 36 pinto beans or sunflower seeds
- potting soil
- 12 paper cups
- saucers
- ruler
- 4 milk cartons
- colored cellophane sheets
- marker
- different light sources: incandescent bulb (regular 60 watt lightbulb), fluorescent bulb (1.2-meter [4-ft] long, 40 watt), and sunlight
- masking tape
- marker
- scissors
- water

# Procedure:

1. Use the same experimental design as in Experiment 2.1, but label the 3 groups of pots s for sunlight, I for incandescent light, and F for fluorescent light. **Have an adult** help you set up the incandescent and fluorescent lights so that both groups are the same distance (about 30 to 46 centimeters [12 to 18 in]) from the light source. Allow the seedlings to grow for two weeks. Water the seedlings when the top 2 centimeters (0.8 in) of soil gets dry.

2. Make the same data collection charts as in Experiment 2.1. Graph your data. Does the *type* of light affect plant growth? If a plant is not growing well, will it respond to a change of light source?

3. Do plants have the same response to different colors of light? Using different colored sheets of plastic cellophane (make sure to include green), you can make frames to cover the young plants. Cut two sides out of each of 4 milk cartons and use masking tape to secure the cellophane around the openings and over the top (see Figure 9). Leave some open space at the bottom of the side openings for gas exchange. Place the plants in the cartons, tape the cellophane tops, and place the cartons near a light source (fluorescent or sunlight). Observe the growth for two weeks. What are the differences in growth? Why do you think green light is not helpful to plants?

## Figure 9.

Cut two sides out of a milk carton and cover the opening with cellophane. Place a plant in the carton, tape cellophane over the top, and keep the carton near a light source (sunlight or fluorescent) for two weeks.

# Results and Conclusions

Plants use the energy in light to power the chemical reaction that allows them to make sugar from water and carbon dioxide. All light is not the same. Light occurs in different colors, or wavelengths, that are not equally useful to plants. Plants use red light (long wavelengths) and blue light (short wavelengths). They also reflect most green light, which is why plants appear green. In addition, the intensity (or brightness) of the light affects plant growth.

 ## Science Project Idea

- A current global problem is the depletion of the ozone layer, a layer in the atmosphere that blocks out ultraviolet (UV) light. Some plants are showing damage from too much UV light. Set up an experiment to test the effect of UV light on plant growth. What parts of Earth are experiencing a growing hole in the ozone layer? Find out what is being done about it by the United States and other countries.

# EXPERIMENT 2.3

## Exercise and Water Requirements

### Question:

Does exercise increase a person's need for water?

### Hypothesis:

Water needs to be replenished after exercise.

## Materials:

- 3 or more people who can exercise two days for at least 45 minutes each day*
- scale to weigh people
- clock
- drinking water
- towel for each person
- 2 changes of clothes for each person

*You need to do this experiment at least two times with each person (once on two different days) to obtain the data to make it reliable. The more you repeat an experiment, the more reliable the data become.*

# Procedure:

1. Weigh each person. They all should be wearing shorts and a T-shirt (no shoes or socks).

2. Have them change into different clothes and exercise (for example, running, playing soccer, lifting weights, walking briskly, skateboarding, or swimming) for at least 45 minutes. The person cannot drink any water during this time.

3. After the exercise, have each person towel off and put on the original shorts and T-shirt (no socks or shoes). Record each person's weight. Once the weighing is complete, have each person drink water to prevent dehydration. How much weight did each person lose? Determine the volume of water that weighs that much.

4. Repeat this procedure on a different day with the same people. Record the results for the participants each of the two times they exercise.

   a. Weight before exercise

   b. Weight after exercise

   c. Total weight loss

   d. Amount of water lost: First determine the weight lost. One pound of water measures 0.5 liter (17 oz). If the person lost 2 pounds, they lost 1 liter (34 oz) of water.

   e. For each of the above (1–4), determine the average for the two days: Add the two weights (or amounts of water) and divide by 2. For example, if a person lost 2 pounds during exercise on day 1 and 3 pounds on day 2, the average water weight lost is:

$$\text{average} = \frac{2 + 3}{2} = \frac{5}{2}, \text{ or 2.5 lbs}$$

# Results and Conclusions

The human body is about 65 percent water. Humans need to consume about 1.5 liters (61 oz) of water a day, more if they are active. The body gains water when a person drinks fluids or eats foods that have a high water content, such as fruits or vegetables.

People excrete water in several ways. One is by urinating. We also lose water every time we breathe out, because the air we exhale contains water vapor. Some water escapes through our skin even if we are not sweating. When we exercise, we lose even more water. We sweat, which our body does to cool off. We also lose more water because breathing increases to provide more oxygen to the cells. Some athletes—and people who work in the heat—will drink two to three times more water than the average person.

The body responds to water loss. It responds without our having to think about it. One response to water loss is that we feel thirsty. This feeling causes us to drink water.

What were the results of your experiment? How much water was lost during exercise? Does temperature affect the amount of water lost during exercise? Do heavier people lose more water than thinner people? Does drinking water before exercise affect water loss? Does a person lose as much water when not exercising? How could you show this and add it to your project data?

#  EXPERIMENT 2.4

## Plants and Nutrients

### Question:

Can plants get food from water?

### Hypothesis:

Plants absorb nutrients from water.

## Materials:

- 1 large plant (geranium, coleus, or spider plant)
- 8 paper cups (to root stems)
- scissors
- 8 plastic 2-liter bottles
- ruler
- 24 pencils or small pieces of dowel
- permanent marker
- distilled water
- plant food
- measuring cup
- tablespoon
- 1-liter bottle for plant food solution
- potting soil
- perlite (sold with potting soils)
- sunny window
- scale
- paper towel
- water

*Note: This project will take three weeks or more.*

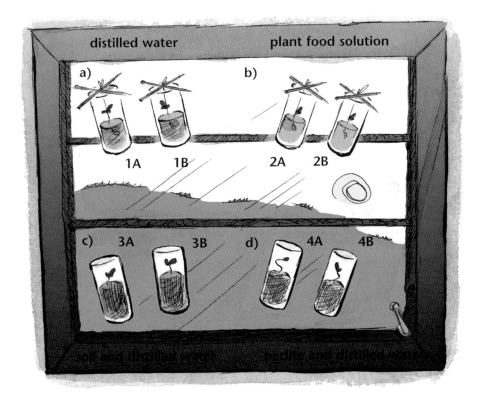

**Figure 10.**

a) Add only distilled water to group #1.
b) Add distilled water with plant food to group #2.
c) Add distilled water to plants in potting soil, group #3.
d) Add distilled water to plants in perlite, group #4.

# Procedure:

1. Obtain a large plant, such as a geranium, a coleus, or a spider plant. Cut eight stems at least 8 centimeters (3 in) long from the plant and put them in water. Allow these cuttings to sit in a paper cup of water until the roots of each stem are over 1 centimeter (0.4 in) long.

2. Carefully cut the top from eight 2-liter bottles, leaving an 18-centimeter-(7-in-) high base. Cut 3 slits near the top of each bottle. Using pencils or dowels, create triangular supports for the cuttings (see Figure 10). Label two bottles 1-A: DISTILLED WATER and 1-B: DISTILLED WATER. Label another two bottles 2-A: PLANT FOOD SOLUTION and 2-B: PLANT FOOD SOLUTION.

3. Fill bottles 1-A and 1-B with distilled water. Mark the water level. Using distilled water, make 1 liter (1 qt) of plant food according to package directions. Fill bottles 2-A and 2-B with the plant food solution. Mark the water level.

4. Fill two bottles with potting soil and label them 3-A: SOIL/DISTILLED WATER and 3-B: SOIL/DISTILLED WATER.

5. Fill two containers with perlite (perlite is a mineral added to soil to increase the air spaces and therefore its ability to hold water; it has no available nutrients). Label them 4-A: PERLITE/DISTILLED WATER and 4-B: PERLITE/DISTILLED WATER.

   You have two plants in each group so that if the two grow very differently, you'll know that something was wrong in the setup and you need to run that group again.

6. Weigh each cutting and record your data in your notebook. Place or plant one cutting in each bottle. Place them all in a sunny window. Keep the water levels constant in groups A and B. Add 2 tablespoons of distilled water to 3-A, 3-B, 4-A, and 4-B when the top 2 centimeters (0.8 in) of the soil or perlite dries out. Keep the water level constant in 1-A and 1-B, and the plant food solution constant in 2-A and 2-B.

7. Make observations on day 1 and on day 14. Record the number of leaves, height, and wet weight for each group and record your results in your science notebook. You can make a table similar to Table 1. (To determine the wet weight of each cutting, remove one plant from each group, and save the other for your science project presentation. Carefully wash the roots and pat the plant dry. Weigh it. This is called

Table 1.

Nutrient Sources and Plant Growth

| Group | Number of Leaves | | Height | | Wet Weight | |
|---|---|---|---|---|---|---|
| | Day 1 | Day 14 | Day 1 | Day 14 | Day 1 | Day 14 |
| Distilled water    1-A | | | | | | |
| 2-A | | | | | | |
| Plant food solution    1-B | | | | | | |
| 2-B | | | | | | |
| Soil with distilled    3-A water | | | | | | |
| 3-B | | | | | | |
| Perlite with distilled    4-A water | | | | | | |
| 4-B | | | | | | |

wet weight because water is still in the plant cells.)

8. Present your data in graph form. Which plants showed the most growth? The least? From where did the plants in each group obtain nutrients? How did the plants in group #3 obtain nutrients from the soil? Were these nutrients available to group #4? Which plants had only the sugars they made in the leaves for growth? Was this sufficient for healthy plant growth?

Do plants grow as well over a long period in just houseplant food solution? Check the ingredients and compare the nutrients to those in a hydroponic solution, which allows you to grow plants without soil. How could you test what nutrients plants need to grow well?

## Figure 11.

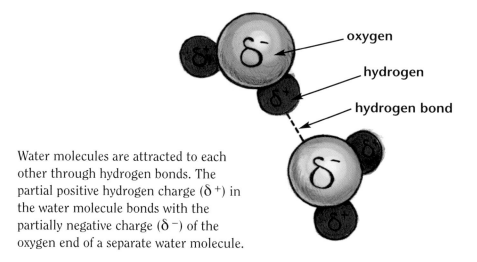

Water molecules are attracted to each other through hydrogen bonds. The partial positive hydrogen charge ($\delta^+$) in the water molecule bonds with the partially negative charge ($\delta^-$) of the oxygen end of a separate water molecule.

# Results and Conclusions

Life on our planet first appeared in what some scientists have called a primordial watery soup. Organisms first lived in water, then they moved from water onto land. When they moved to land, they had to evolve ways of taking water with them. Plants need water to transport nutrients throughout the plant, to regulate temperature, and to metabolize food. They also need water for photosynthesis and to keep stiffness (turgor) in their leaves. Without enough water, plant cells stop functioning and the plant dies.

So what is this substance that covers two-thirds of our planet and fills over half a person's body? Water is a unique molecule of two atoms of hydrogen bonded to one atom of oxygen. Because of the arrangement of atoms, the oxygen end of the molecule has a slight negative charge, and the hydrogen ends have slight positive charges (see Figure 11). This makes water a polar molecule—it has a positive pole and a negative pole. Therefore, water attracts some substances, such as sugars, and repels others, such as waxes and oils. In plants, polarity allows water to move upward in the stem because it sticks to the inside of the tubes inside the plant stem. Water also moves up because it is pulled by evaporation. Water can dissolve many substances, such as nutrients and gases. Once dissolved, the nutrients and gases can be transported in and out of cell membranes.

Science Project Idea

- Different types of plants have different nutrient needs. Plants need nitrogen for making chlorophyll and many other growth processes. Too much nitrogen can cause some plants to die. Design some experiments to determine plant responses to differing amounts of nitrogen (using fertilizers). Include corn, beans, and sunflowers. Experiment with applications of micronutrients (such as iron), which are necessary in small quantities but toxic in larger amounts.

# EXPERIMENT 2.5

## Plant Growth and Oxygen

### Question:

What gas does a germinating seed need to grow?

### Hypothesis:

Germinating seeds need oxygen to grow.

### Materials:

- **an adult**
- 30 pinto beans (available as dried beans in the grocery store)
- bowl or cup of water
- perlite (sold with potting soils)
- measuring cup
- ruler
- 2 plates
- 2 tea light candles
- 2 wide mouthed glass jars
- masking tape
- marker
- matches

## Procedure:

1. Soak 30 pinto beans overnight in water to soften the seed coat. Soak 1 cup of perlite in 2 cups of water overnight so that the perlite will be fully saturated.

2. Put 2 centimeters (⅔ in) of perlite on 2 plates and ¼ cup of water or enough so that there is some water on each plate. Put a small tea light on each plate.

3. Spread 15 seeds over the perlite on each plate, fairly close to the tea light (see Figure 12).

4. Label a widemouthed glass jar JAR #1 and place it over the unlit candle and the 15 seeds, making sure the lip of the jar is against the plate. Label a second jar JAR #2. **Have an adult** light the candle on the second plate, and place Jar #2 over the seeds and the candle.

5. When the candle goes out, what gas is no longer present in the bottle? For ten days, record your observations about the length of the sprouts and the number of leaves in each jar. Which seedlings grew the most? Why do you think the seedlings in one jar grew better than the other?

## Results and Conclusions

Plants, just like animals, need a steady supply of oxygen. Plants use oxygen to break down and use the materials they need to grow. A sprouting seed does not yet have leaves with which to make food. Therefore, it does not need carbon dioxide, because it does not perform photosynthesis. (Remember, photosynthesis takes place in the leaves.) All of the young plant's food is stored as sugars inside the seed. To grow leaves, the seedling first must break down the sugars inside the seed.

Figure 12.

Spread 15 seeds on each plate of perlite and water. Place an unlit candle on one and have an adult light a candle on the other plate. Cover the candles and seeds with widemouthed jars.

## Science Project Ideas

- Repeat the experiment, but use small plants in potting soil instead of seeds in perlite. Record your observations each day for ten days. Did the plants grow as well in the same conditions as the seedlings? Why or why not? In the jar with the candle that burned, where does the plant get oxygen to use during the night? Could **an adult** test to see if the jar with the candle got a new supply of oxygen? (Hint: Light a long match and quickly put it in the jar.)

- Using a solution of bromthymol blue (see Appendix), a jar with a lid, and 30 pinto beans that have been soaked overnight in water, design an experiment **under adult supervision** to determine if these sprouting seeds give off carbon dioxide. What would happen if you added a small plant to the container? How about several snails?

# EXPERIMENT 2.6

## Plants, Carbon Dioxide, and Photosynthesis

### Question:

Can you show that plants use carbon dioxide during photosynthesis?

### Hypothesis:

Bromthymol blue, which detects the presence of carbon dioxide, can be used to test if plants use carbon dioxide during photosynthesis.

### Materials:

- **an adult**
- 8 plastic 1-liter soda bottles
- scissors
- bromthymol blue solution (see Appendix)
- **safety glasses**
- disposable gloves
- straws
- plastic wrap
- tape
- ruler
- clock or watch with second hand
- 4 pieces of elodea (from a fish store or pond)
- water
- well-lit area
- dark cupboard or closet
- permanent marker

*Note: Be careful not to spill the bromthymol blue solution. It can irritate your skin and may stain fabric and rugs. Wear safety glasses and disposable gloves.*

# Procedure:

1. With scissors, cut 8 plastic 1-liter bottles so that there is room to add a plant from the top. **Put on safety glasses and gloves**. Completely fill each bottle with a solution of bromthymol blue, which turns yellow when carbon dioxide is present. With a permanent marker, label the bottles A, B, C, D, E, F, G, and H.

2. To add carbon dioxide to bottle A, **have an adult** gently blow into the solution with a straw until it turns yellow. Make sure you clock the amount of time the adult actually exhales into the straw (see Figure 13). Record the exhale time in your science notebook.

3. Add a 13-centimeter (5-in) piece of elodea to bottle A. Cover the bottle with plastic wrap and tape. Record the color of the solution in bottle A. (This is your 0-minute observation; see Table 2.)

4. Repeat this procedure for bottles B, E, and F. Make sure **the adult** blows for the same amount of time into each bottle.

5. Repeat the procedure for bottles C, D, G, and H. But, this time, do not add any plants to these four bottles. These bottles are your controls (no plants). Record the color of the solution in each bottle for your 0-minute observation (see Table 2).

6. Place bottles A, B, C, and D in a dark cupboard at room temperature. Place bottles E, F, G, and H in a well-lit (but not hot) area. Record the color changes and check for the presence of gas bubbles every 30 minutes for the next 90 minutes.

   Which plants used no carbon dioxide? How do you know? In which bottles was there a change of color? In which bottles did you observe gas bubbles? What gas, do you think, caused these bubbles?

Figure 13.

Fill eight bottles with bromthymol blue solution. **Have an adult** gently blow through a straw into the solution until it turns yellow. **Warning: Do not inhale the solution.** Add pieces of elodea to bottles A, B, E, and F.

## Table 2.

## Carbon Dioxide Uptake by Elodea
## Growing in Bromthymol Blue Solution

| Color Changes/Presence of Bubbles | | | | |
|---|---|---|---|---|
| Bottle | 0 minutes | 30 minutes | 60 minutes | 90 minutes |
| A (dark/elodea) | | | | |
| B (dark/elodea) | | | | |
| C (dark/no plants) | | | | |
| D (dark/no plants) | | | | |
| E (light/elodea) | | | | |
| F (light/elodea) | | | | |
| G (light/no plants) | | | | |
| H (light/no plants) | | | | |

# Results and Conclusions

Plants are the primary producers on the planet. Primary producers can make their own food. Plants make food in cells called chloroplasts, which contain chlorophyll. By absorbing the energy from sunlight, plants are able to break apart water and carbon dioxide and build sugar molecules. This process is called photosynthesis. During photosynthesis, plants release oxygen. In aquatic plants, gas bubbles can be seen escaping from the leaves during the day.

What were the results of your experiment? Can you extend the experiment to determine if the color will change from yellow to blue at a different rate with less light or with more light? Do all plants photosynthesize, and therefore use carbon dioxide, at the same rate? At night, many plants do not photosynthesize, but instead use oxygen (and give off carbon dioxide). How could you test this?

 Science Project Idea

- Fruits give off a gas called ethylene that is responsible for fruit ripening and falling from the plant. Design several experiments to see the effects of ethylene gas on ripe and unripe fruit.

# CHAPTER 3

# Behavioral and Physiological Responses of Plants and Animals

After running five kilometers (3.1 mi), would you put on a thick jacket or drink a glass of water? If it were 38°C (100°F) outside and you had no hat or water, would you sit in the sun or the shade? How you react to an environmental change is called a response. Organisms respond to stimuli, such as heat, cold, or noise, in order to keep themselves alive. The response can be a change in behavior or in physiology (body processes). The response regulates such things as temperature, water, and nutrient levels in the plant or animal. This process of adjusting to one's surroundings is called homeostasis—it is an

◄ When a camel crosses the desert, its body processes must adjust to the intense heat to survive.

attempt to maintain equilibrium. If an organism does not make the right adjustments, its cells might freeze, overheat, starve, or dehydrate. The organism will then die.

Some animal responses are behavioral, such as drinking water or moving into the sun to get warm. Some responses are physiological, such as when a dog pants.

Plants do not have brains or sensory organs, but they do have chemical substances called hormones that can regulate their responses to light, touch, and even gravity. These responses are called tropisms, or movements. Plants respond to light (phototropism), touch (thigmotropism), and gravity (gravitropism).

# EXPERIMENT 3.1

## Plant Growth Response to Light

### Question:
How does light affect the direction of plant growth?

### Hypothesis:
Plants grow in the direction of a light source.

### Materials:
- 16 sunflower seeds
- 4 plastic pots
- potting soil
- 4 saucers or lids to fit under the pots
- permanent marker
- ruler
- water
- overhead light source (fluorescent light or natural lighting that is away from direct sunlight)
- sunny window
- camera (optional)

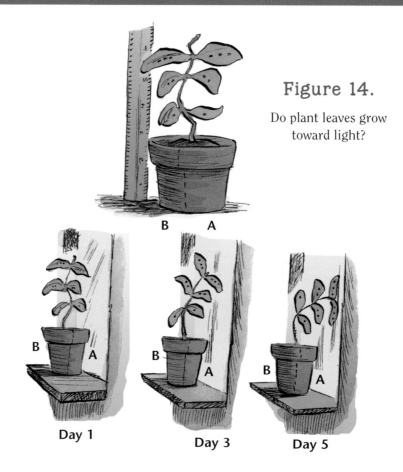

**Figure 14.**

Do plant leaves grow
toward light?

B    A

B    A    Day 1

B    A    Day 3

B    A    Day 5

# Procedure:

1. Fill 4 plastic pots with potting soil. Place the pots on 4 saucers or lids to collect any drainage water. Plant 4 sunflower seeds in each pot and water the pots. Let them grow under an overhead light source until there are at least six healthy leaves on each plant. Add water when the top 2 centimeters (0.8 in) of the soil are dry.

2. Use a permanent marker to mark one side of each pot with an A and the other side with a B (see Figure 14). Use the marker to mark the tips of three leaves on both the A and B sides with tiny dots: mark one leaf with 1 dot, one leaf with 2 dots, and one leaf with 3 dots. For each of the 6 marked leaves, measure and record the distance from the leaf to the surface on which the cup sits. You can take a photo at each stage, including the measurements, for a science project.

3. Place two plants in a sunny window with side B facing away from the window. Place two pots in a place with no direct light (away from any windows). For each plant, measure and record the distance of the six marked leaves from the surface on which the cup sits (Day 1). Also record this measurement for each plant on Day 3 and Day 5.

## Results and Conclusions

When light conditions are low, the plant releases auxin, a type of hormone. Auxin causes the cells on the dark side of the plant to grow longer—making the dark side bend toward the light. Plants also grow leaves in a pattern that allows for the most exposure to sunlight.

In your experiment, did the leaves move? If so, in what direction did they move? Was there leaf movement in the set of plants placed away from direct sunlight? Why or why not? What happens if you turn the plants near the window around? Do different types of plants react to light at the same rate? How does the intensity (brightness), the type of light, or the age of the plant affect any movement?

Science Project Ideas

- **With an adult,** walk in a forest and look for signs of trees growing toward the sunlight. Look for trees with curved trunks growing on a slope or from rocks. Some trees (especially aspens and birches) become bent over by the weight of snow. Why do the trees grow upward again in the spring? Can you design an experiment to demonstrate the ability of a plant to grow upright? Try using tomato or coleus plants growing from containers tipped on their sides.

- Grow some mung beans or alfalfa sprouts (seeds and directions are available at health food stores). Grow one jar in the dark and one in the light. Low light availability affects not only the look of the plant but also the starch/sugar content. **Have an adult** help you use iodine to see which plants contain more starch. Why do people who grow sprouts for food grow them in the dark?

# EXPERIMENT 3.2

## Food and Water Movement in Land Plants

### Question:

How do land plants transport food and water?

### Hypothesis:

Land plants transport food and water through roots and capillaries.

## Materials:

- sugar
- green food coloring
- salt
- red food coloring
- 2 glasses
- 4 celery stalks with leaves
- hot tap water
- sunny area
- butter knife
- ruler
- measuring cups
- measuring spoons
- vegetable peeler
- magnifying glass
- masking tape
- permanent marker

## Procedure:

1. Add 1 cup of hot tap water, 1 tablespoon of sugar, and 3 drops of green food coloring to a clear drinking glass labeled #1.

2. In a glass labeled #2, dissolve 2 teaspoons of salt and 3 drops of red food coloring in 1 cup of hot tap water.

3. Use a butter knife to carefully cut 2 centimeters (0.8 in) from the tops of four stalks of celery. Do any of the pieces taste salty or sweet? Now place 2 stalks of celery in each glass in a sunny spot. Look at the celery and measure how far up the celery stalk the water has moved after 12, 24, 36, and 48 hours.

4. Remove the celery stalks. Use a butter knife to carefully cut a 2-centimeter (0.8-in) piece from the top of each stalk. Do any of the pieces taste salty or sweet now? How did the sugar and salt get transported to the top of the celery stalk?

5. Using a vegetable peeler, carefully cut a very thin slice from the middle of a piece of colored celery stalk. Look at it with a magnifying glass and make a diagram of what you see. Can you see the colored tubes? These are the transport vessels of the plant.

   Can you affect the rate of transport by increasing the pull of evaporation (such as by increasing the heat source or air movement)? Will water move at a different rate if the leaves are taken off the celery first? If you start with limp celery (most of the water has left the cells), will the water travel more quickly than if you begin with stiff celery?

# Results and Conclusions

Most plants can make their own food, which is either used or stored in leaves or roots. To make food through photosynthesis, plants need water. To grow, they also need the nutrients (such as nitrogen, phosphorus, and iron) dissolved in the water. Many plants grow a vast network of roots to increase their contact with water and the nutrients dissolved in the water.

Once water is absorbed through the roots, it moves throughout the plant via small tubes called capillaries. The process is called capillarity. The water moves in two ways: Water sticks to the sides of tiny capillaries in the plant, and water is pulled up by evaporation.

 Science Project Idea

- Can you get a white flower to turn red or green? How could you create green, red, and blue stripes in a white flower? Can you change the color of a rooted plant's flowers or only cut flowers? Will all substances be transported? Dissolve different substances in water and try it. You can try chocolate, brown sugar, molasses, or mustard.

# EXPERIMENT 3.3

## Ants, Energy, and Food

### Question:

Do ants appear to conserve energy when finding food sources?

### Hypothesis:

Ants work together to carry food back to the colony.

### Materials:

- an active anthill
- tape measure
- bread or cookie crumbs
- clock or watch

# Procedure:

1. Find an anthill with ants working. Be careful not to disturb it in any way. Place a small pile of cookie or bread crumbs about 1 meter (3 ft) from the anthill. Draw a map of the anthill and the crumb pile location. Record the amount of time it takes for the first ant to discover and carry off a crumb.

2. During the next twenty minutes, count the number of ants at the pile. Mark the ants' general route on your map.

   Does the number of ants at the pile increase over time? Do the ants take the longest or shortest route back and forth from the anthill? Do ants show any patterns of movement that make good use of their energies for finding food? Is there an advantage to this type of behavior?

3. Next, move the pile of crumbs to a different location. Do not harm any ants or let them get on you. Make the same recordings and observations for the next twenty minutes.

4. Present your data using a line graph (see Figure 15).

## Figure 15.

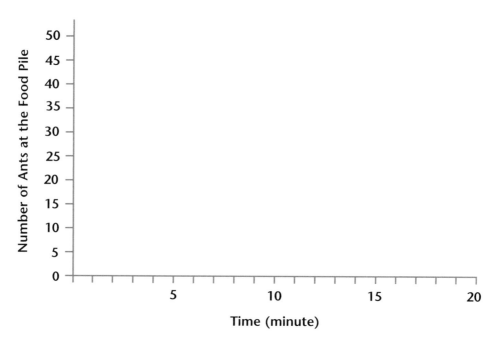

**Number of Ants at Food Pile Over Time**

Plot the number of ants that find the food (x-axis) over time (y-axis). Connect the points to make a line graph.

# Results and Conclusions

Ants follow paths laid down for them by other ants. When an ant finds food it lays a path for other ants to follow. When another ant finds the path, it will be able to find the food.

What happens if you leave a tiny trail of crumbs marking a longer route to the pile? Will the ants create a shorter route back to the anthill once the crumbs on the longer route are gone?

 Science Project Idea

- Observing squirrel activities at different times of the year requires planning ahead. In the autumn, record the number of trips a squirrel makes to collect seeds (acorns, pinecones) in one hour. Do this for several days. Make the same observations in the same area at another time of year. Is there a difference in activity level? What behavior is the squirrel exhibiting in the autumn? Is this activity seen in the winter or spring? What other animals can you observe storing food?

#  EXPERIMENT 3.4

## Gas Exchange in Plants

### Question:

Can you observe how plants exchange gases with the environment?

### Hypothesis:

Stomata and guard cells in a plant's leaf can be manipulated and observed.

### Materials:

- tweezers
- kalanchoe plant (in most grocery stores)
- slide
- coverslip
- salt
- teaspoon
- compound microscope with light source
- measuring cup
- eyedropper
- petroleum jelly
- warm water

## Procedure:

1. With tweezers, peel off the outer layer (epidermis) of a kalanchoe leaf. Place the layer on a slide with a coverslip. Using a compound microscope with light source, find the stomata (openings) and the guard cells (see Figure 16). Stomata are round openings surrounded by doughnut-shaped guard cells. Guard cells contain chloroplasts, which are green. Diagram and label what you observe.

## Figure 16.

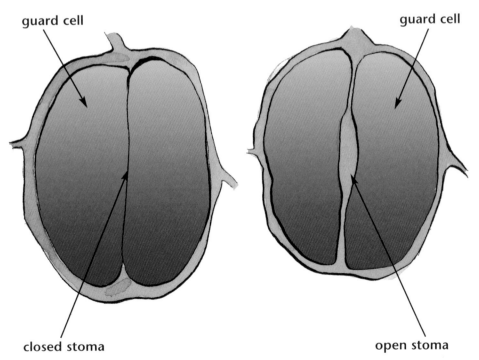

guard cell

guard cell

closed stoma

open stoma

Stomata and guard cells regulate water movement in and out of leaves.

2. Dissolve ¼ teaspoon of salt in ¼ cup of warm water. Add a drop of this salt solution to the slide right next to the coverslip. Using a microscope, observe what happens as the water seeps into the cells.

As the guard cells lose water, they collapse and the stomata close. The difference in salt concentration causes water to move from a lower concentration solution in the guard cell to a higher concentration solution outside the cell in the salt solution. When guard cells absorb water and swell, they move apart. This opens the stomata.

3. Is there gas exchange through the stomata? To find out, coat some of the leaves on the live kalanchoe with petroleum jelly to plug the openings. What do you think will happen to the leaf? What would happen if you coated more than one leaf or the stem?

# Results and Conclusions

Plants have tiny openings on their leaves, which are called stomata (singular is *stoma*). Guard cells open and close the stomata to control the flow of gases in and out of a plant. The stomata open and close depending on the time of day and the weather conditions.

Plants need both carbon dioxide and oxygen for their life functions. They use carbon dioxide during photosynthesis to make simple sugars. But they need oxygen, just as animals do, when they are breaking down sugars to produce energy. And just as animals do, plants also give off carbon dioxide during this time. Most plants give off carbon dioxide at night.

## Science Project Ideas

- Do aquatic plants have stomata? Why or why not? Design an experiment to test your hypothesis.

- Design an experiment to reverse the times when the stomata in a plant are open and closed.

# EXPERIMENT 3.5

## Exercise, Gas Exchange, and Heart Rate

### Question:

Does exercise increase a person's heart rate and therefore rate of gas exchange?

### Hypothesis:

Heart rate increases during exercise to carry more oxygen to the blood.

### Materials:

- 3 or more people who can exercise for two minutes at a time
- stopwatch, or clock with a second hand

## Procedure:

1. Ask three or more people to participate in an experiment on exercising. But do not give any details of the experiment, as this may affect their behavior. Test each person separately.

2. Have one person remain in a resting state (sitting quietly) for at least 10 minutes. Then have the person count the number of times her heart beats in 60 seconds. (Have her put a hand on her chest until she feels her heart beating, then you can begin timing). While the person is counting heartbeats, you count the number of breaths she takes (a breath is one inhale and one exhale). Do not tell her you are counting her breaths, as this may affect the result.

3. Have the person rest for 2 more minutes and then again record the number of heartbeats and breaths for 60 seconds. Repeat this with two more people (remember, the more subjects you have, the more reliable your data).

   **Note:** *This part of the experiment is set up so that you are recording the person's resting heartbeat and breathing rate in the same way as you will in the following parts of the experiment.*

4. Now, have one person at a time exercise for 2 minutes (run quickly in place, climb stairs, or do jumping jacks). Immediately have the person record the number of her heartbeats for 60 seconds. While the person is counting her heartbeats, observe and count the number of breaths she takes during that minute.

## Figure 17.

## Effect of Exercise on Heartbeat and Number of Breaths Per Minute

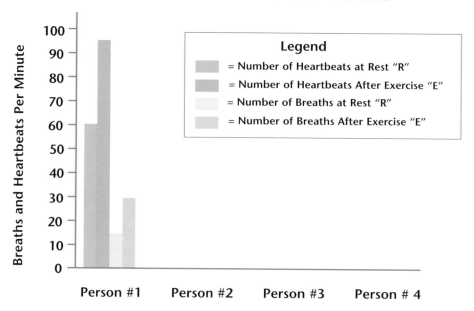

You can make a bar graph to record heart rate and breathing rate in response to exercise.

5. After 2 more minutes of the same exercise, record the number of heart-beats and breaths taken in 60 seconds. Why does exercise increase the heart rate and the breathing rate? Repeat this experiment.

6. Graph your results (see Figure 17).

How does a body respond to the increased need for oxygen to break down sugars for energy? In which state (resting or exercising) did the body exhale more carbon dioxide? How do you know?

Why do people have different biological responses to exercise? How long does it take each person to return to the resting heartbeat and breathing level? Repeat the experiment comparing a person who exercises regularly and someone who does not. Why are the heart rates so different? (**Hint:** *The heart is a muscle. The more use it gets, the stronger and more efficiently it pumps.*)

# Results and Conclusions

When you exercise, your body needs extra energy to work the muscles. The more energy you use, the more oxygen you need. Animals have mechanisms to control the flow of gases in their systems depending on their gas needs. Increased breathing brings more oxygen into the body. In the lungs, oxygen attaches to the red blood cells. The stronger and faster the heart beats, the more blood is circulated from the lungs throughout the body, which means more oxygen gets delivered. Once the oxygen is delivered to the cells in the body, the deoxygenated blood (blood without oxygen) is pumped back to the lungs, where it absorbs more oxygen.

# EXPERIMENT 3.6

## Seedlings and Cold Temperatures

### Question:

How do seedlings respond to cold temperatures?

### Hypothesis:

Seedlings may not germinate or grow when the temperature is too cold.

### Materials:

- cold cabbage seeds or broccoli seeds
- 6 paper cups
- scissors
- saucers
- potting soil
- cooler
- meterstick or yardstick
- water
- fluorescent light or sunny window
- permanent marker
- outdoor thermometer
- ice packs or block of ice
- freezer
- clock

## Procedure:

1. Use scissors to poke three holes in the bottom of each of six paper cups. Plant 3 cabbage or broccoli seeds in each cup. Place the cups on saucers and place them about 45 centimeters (18 in) beneath a fluorescent light or in a sunny window.

2. Water the cups throughout the experiment when the top 2 centimeters (0.8 in) of the soil gets dry.

3. When the seedlings are about 2.5 centimeters (1 in) tall, remove all but the healthiest one (tallest, greenest, most leaves) from each cup.

4. Divide the cups into two groups. Label one group H for hardened off, and one group N for not hardened off. *Hardening off* refers to becoming accustomed to colder temperatures. Why can't you buy the seedlings from a nursery for this experiment?

5. Allow the N group to keep growing in the light. Using a cooler, an outdoor thermometer, and a block of ice or ice packs, add ice to make the cooler 4°C (40°F). Take the seedlings in the H group and expose them to the following temperatures for the specified amount of time:

   Day 1: 4°C (40°F) for 1 hour

   Day 2: 4°C (40°F) for 2 hours

   Day 3: 4°C (40°F) for 3 hours

   Day 4: 1°C (34°F) (add more ice to the cooler) for 2 hours

   Day 5: 1°C (34°F) for 3 hours

   Day 6: 1°C (34°F) for 5 hours

   Day 7: 1°C (34°F) for 5 hours

During this week, only water the plants in the H group half as much as you have been. When the H group is not in the cooler, put the pots next to the N group in the light.

6. After one week, place two cups from each group in the freezer overnight. (Keep the other two plant cups for your science fair presentation.)

7. Wait several days, or until you see a change in the plants. Keep a chart of the exposure temperatures, times, and amount of water given in your project. Did any of the plants die? Why did you need to decrease the water as you hardened off the seedlings? (**Hint:** *Think about what happens to water when it freezes.*) Does it make a difference if you do not decrease the water? Can all seedlings be hardened off? Try the experiment with tomato, lettuce, and spinach plants.

## Results and Conclusions

Plants, like animals, respond to changes in temperature. In colder weather, all chemical processes (such as metabolism) slow down. Some plants respond by not germinating or not growing in cold weather. Other plants have adapted to survive in colder weather conditions.

# EXPERIMENT 3.7

## Exercise and Muscle Growth

### Question:

How can you cause muscles to grow?

### Hypothesis:

Muscle mass can be added through weight lifting.

### Materials:

- 3 people who can lift free weights (they can be light weight—even 2-pound weights will work)
- **an adult**
- tape measure
- free weights

Figure 18.

a)

b)

a) First measure the circumference of the relaxed upper arm.
b) Then measure the circumference of the flexed upper arm.

# Procedure:

1. Find three volunteers who would like to participate in the experiment. Explain that it will involve arm exercises and recording muscle growth.

2. The procedure is the same for each volunteer: With a tape measure, measure the circumference of the upper arm at its largest point (the distance around the upper arm, which includes the biceps and triceps muscles) in a resting state (see Figure 18a). Then have her bend the elbow and make a fist to flex the muscles (see Figure 18b). Measure the same place on the flexed upper arm. Record the measurements of the upper arm both at rest and flexed.

3. **Under adult supervision**, have the volunteers find suitable free weights. They should be able to lift the weights easily at first, then after doing 10 curls (raising the weight to shoulder level by contracting the biceps muscle) the muscle should feel tired. Be careful, because if the weight is too heavy, you can damage your ligaments (what connects your muscles to your bones).

4. For the next three weeks, have the volunteers do the following every other day: three sets of 15 curls on each arm. Have each person rest for one minute between each set of 15 curls. It is important to rest a day in between while the muscle heals. Exercise actually breaks down the muscle, which is why it gets sore. As the muscle heals, it grows stronger.

5. Every fourth day, measure and record the upper arm circumference both at rest and flexed. At the end of three weeks, record the final muscle size.

6. Present the data on a graph. Did exercise make the muscles grow larger? What are two ways in which you could affect the rate at which muscles develop?

# Results and Conclusions

Growth, for both plants and animals, involves taking simple materials from the environment (nutrients and vitamins) and reorganizing them into more complex molecules. These larger molecules are then used to repair cells or to make new cells. This process is called metabolism, and it requires energy and food. Some cells, such as bone cells, continue to multiply as you grow.

Muscles in animals get bigger when protein is added to each muscle cell. Muscle cells, also called muscle fibers, are shaped like cylinders. Muscles extend from one end of the bone to the other. They are attached to the bones by ligaments. Repeated stretching puts stress on the muscle and leads to more protein synthesis and muscle growth.

The actual number of muscle cells a person has never increases. The number is determined by one's genetics. Those born with more are often called "natural athletes."

# EXPERIMENT 3.8

## The Changing Shape of Plant Cells

### Question:

How can you cause plant cells to elongate?

### Hypothesis:

Plant cells may elongate during growth.

### Materials:

- 18 bean seeds
- 9 paper cups
- scissors
- saucers
- potting soil
- fluorescent light
- permanent marker
- 2 windows: one sunny, one with indirect sun
- auxin (from nursery or garden shop)
- cotton swabs
- ruler
- water

## Procedure:

1. Use scissors to poke three holes in the bottom of each of nine paper cups. Fill the cups with potting soil and plant two bean seeds in each. Place the cups, on saucers, 30 to 46 centimeters (12 to 18 in) from a fluorescent light source or in a window that does not receive direct sunlight. Water the plants when the soil gets dry.

2. When the plants are 2.5 centimeters (1 in) tall, remove one plant from each pot, leaving the healthier plant (the one that is greener and has more leaves). With a marker, label three pots w for "window" and place them near a sunny window. Do not move them.

3. Mark three cups E for "even lighting," and place them away from any strong light source. For example, place them in a window that does not receive direct sunlight.

4. Mark three paper cups E/A for "even lighting with auxin." On the side of the paper cup with the label, apply some auxin with a cotton swab to only the middle part of the stem on that side (see Figure 19). Then place these three plants next to the E plants. Observe the growth during the next 5 days.

   Which set of plants grew in the same way? What do the W plants have in common with the E/A plants? If the W plants bent over, where did they get the auxin necessary to bend? Did the plants in the E group bend?

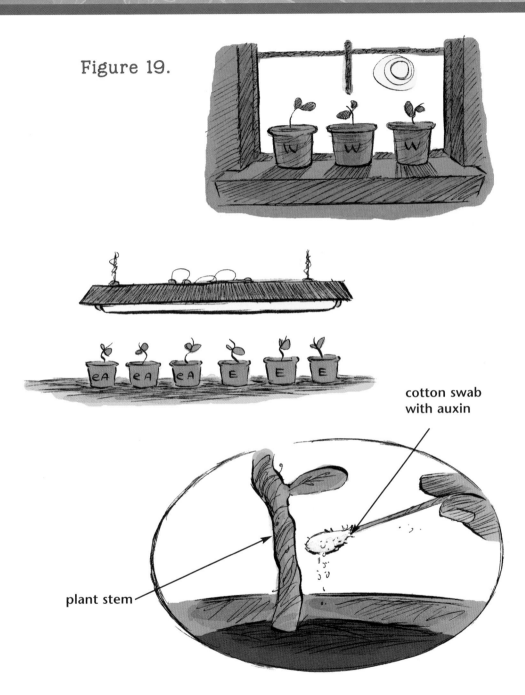

Figure 19.

cotton swab
with auxin

plant stem

Place three plants (W) near a sunny window, three plants (E) under an overhead light source, and three plants (E/A) next to them. With a cotton swab, apply auxin to one side of the stem of each E/A plant. Observe the plant growth for five days.

# Results and Conclusions

Plants contain hormones, which are growth-regulating chemicals. One plant hormone is called auxin. Auxin promotes growth in both stems and roots. It usually stimulates cells to elongate, or to get longer. This causes one side of a plant to grow longer, which causes the plant to bend toward the light. The presence of auxin controls the growth of the seedling. The stem grows up toward the light and the roots grow down into the soil. Auxin has other effects on plant development. It is responsible for the branching out of roots, the growth of fruits, and the growth of xylem and phloem tissue (the tubes that carry food and water throughout the plant).

How did auxin affect the way the plants grew in your experiment? How could you make the plant stems in the E group bend? What happens if you apply auxin to the part of the stem exposed to direct sunlight on the W plant? How could you test to see which part of a plant stores and releases the auxin? (**Hint:** *What happens if you keep taking off the tip of the plant? In what shape does it grow?*) Can you make a plant grow to one side and then to the other?

## Science Project Idea

- Explore the effects of root hormones. These can be purchased at a garden center. Using bean plants, observe the growth differences with and without root hormones. Measure the root growth by obtaining weight and length measurements. Compare the percentage of the plant that is roots in each sample.

## CHAPTER 4

# Plant and Animal Adaptations

With only what you are wearing right now, how long would you survive standing next to an emperor penguin at –40°C (–40°F) in windy Antarctica? If you guessed "not long" (as in minutes), you are right. If you were riding a camel through a hot desert dressed as you are right now, would you or the camel survive longer? Who would survive a twenty-minute dive under freezing water: you or a seal?

So why wouldn't you survive in places that a penguin, a camel, or a seal can? It is because human bodies are not adapted to survive extreme temperatures or to hold their breath for very long.

◀ Penguins developed several adaptations to survive the extreme cold of Antarctica, such as their stiff, densely packed feathers and a thick layer of fat.

Adaptations are changes made over time to allow an organism to survive. It can be a very specific change, as in the development of a bird's bill that allows it to spear fish, or it can be a general change, as when a whole group of animals, such as reptiles, developed scales to prevent water loss through the skin.

Plants also adapt to environments. Some plants can survive three years in a desert without water, while others, such as seaweeds, live in the water all the time. Some plants, such as sundews and pitcher plants, can grow in soils low in nitrogen because they have a special adaptation of trapping and digesting insects to obtain the nitrogen they need to grow.

Why can humans live in almost every habitat, even without biological adaptations, such as a thick layer of fat or feathers for warmth or huge ears to cool themselves? It's something to think about!

# EXPERIMENT 4.1

## Bird Bills and Food Gathering

### Question:

Are certain tools more useful for gathering different foods?

### Hypothesis:

Certain tools are better suited for picking up certain objects.

### Materials:

- 3 people
- various types of seeds, nuts, and soft fruits
- bark
- raisins
- cooked spaghetti (several pieces)
- container of sand
- bowl of water
- duckweed or green leaves
- coffee grounds or tea leaves
- plate
- dried leaves from the ground
- nutcracker
- hand drill
- tea strainer or sieve
- straw
- tweezers
- clawed hammer
- sticky tape
- paper
- piece of cooked chicken

Figure 20.

Assemble a collection of seeds, nuts, leaves, and other possible foods for birds. Gather tools that mimic different bird bills: tweezers, a strainer, a straw, a claw hammer, and a nutcracker.

## Procedure:

1. Place a group of potential bird foods on a table. Include several kinds of nuts, acorns, kernels of corn, soft fruits, various seeds, and a piece of cooked chicken. Find some bark and hide some raisins in it to serve as insect grubs. Bury pieces of cooked spaghetti in a container of sand to serve as worms. Either place some duckweed in a bowl of water or cut up green leaves into tiny pieces to float on the water. Spread some coffee grounds or tea leaves on a plate to serve as insects. Cover them with leaves from the ground.

2. On a table, place some of the following tools for food gathering: a nutcracker, a hand drill, a tea strainer or a small sieve, a straw (like a hummingbird's sipping bill), tweezers, a clawed hammer, and a strip of paper with sticky tape to serve as a bird's tongue (like a woodpecker's). The tools will function in similar ways to birds' bills.

3. Use the following procedure for each of the three people participating. One person at a time enters the room. The person will use one tool at a time and attempt to "eat" (pick up) as many foods as possible (see Figure 20). Each person will have only two attempts at each food with one tool. For example, a person will have only two attempts with a pair of tweezers to open a nut. Then the person must move on to a new food with the tool.

4. Record the results in your science notebook. You can make a table similar to Table 3.

Was each tool well adapted for acquiring each type of food (were the people successful in obtaining the food with it)? Which tool type proved to be the most specific (it obtained the least amount of food)? The most generalized (it obtained the most kinds of foods)?

## Table 3.
## Number of Foods Successfully Obtained

| | Strainer | Nutcracker | Tweezers | Hand drill | Claw of hammer | Straw | Sticky tape |
|---|---|---|---|---|---|---|---|
| Person #1 | | | | | | | |
| Person #2 | | | | | | | |
| Person #3 | | | | | | | |

# Results and Conclusions

Birds have evolved special bill adaptations for obtaining food. Different bird bills can chisel, spear, tear, crack, strain, or probe to help the bird get food. Raptors, such as eagles, hawks, and owls, have strong, hooked bills adapted to tear flesh. Birds that eat seeds, such as finches, have short, thick bills for cracking hulls. Woodpeckers have bills designed to drill holes in wood, where insect prey hides. Hummingbirds have long, thin bills adapted for reaching nectar in the middle of flowers. These special adaptations allow birds to survive in many different habitats—forests, fields, shores, and even mud. Can you imagine how a pelican, with its bill adapted for scooping fish out of the water, could get food from a field? Bird bills are specially designed tools for food collection.

Consider that each tool used in the experiment is similar to different birds' bills. Can you predict a habitat in which each bill type (tool) would be successful or would fail? Could you design a more versatile bill? What problems can you predict for a bird with a bill that isn't designed to obtain food from a certain habitat? What would happen to the bird if it could not move to a different habitat?

# EXPERIMENT 4.2

## Plants and Water Conservation

### Question:

Can you observe different plants' ability to retain water?

### Hypothesis:

By sealing plants in plastic, their ability to retain water can be observed.

### Materials:

- **an adult**
- 2 succulent plants (such as a jade or an aloe)
- 2 leafy plants without waxy leaves (such as a coleus)
- 4 clear plastic bags (produce bags would work well)
- tape
- sunny window
- humidity indicator cards (10–60%); (see Appendix)
- water
- aluminum foil
- scale
- oven
- oven mitts
- magnifying glass or microscope

# Procedure:

1. Obtain two leafy plants and two succulent plants. All four plants should be similar in size. Make sure the soil is moist in each pot.

2. Position a humidity index card next to the leaves and cover each plant with a clear plastic bag (see Figure 21). Tape the bottom of the bag so that it closes around the base of the stem. Place the plants in a sunny window. The humidity index card is sensitive to the amount of moisture in the air.

3. In your science notebook, record the percentage of humidity for each plant every hour for 8 hours in a table similar to Table 4.

4. Make a graph of your data. Did the plants lose the same amount of water, or did one group conserve water (meaning the water was kept in the plant and not released as vapor)? If you had put the plastic bag around the pot also, what water loss would be measured?

5. Examine each type of leaf with a magnifying glass. How do you think leaf structure affects the rate of water loss?

6. Take six leaves from the leafy plant and a small piece of the succulent and place them on separate pieces of aluminum foil. Record the weight of the foil with the six leaves. Do the same for the piece of the succulent. These are their wet weights.

7. **Have an adult**, using oven mitts, bake both samples, still on the foil, in an oven at 250°F (121°C) for about an hour or until the leaves are crumbly. Reweigh the samples. These are their dry weights.

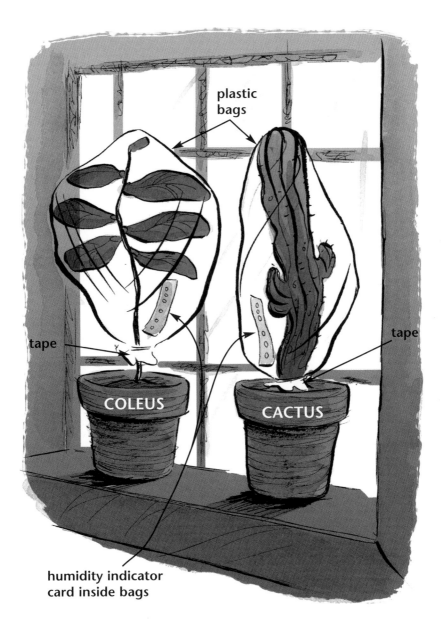

plastic
bags

tape

COLEUS

CACTUS

tape

humidity indicator
card inside bags

## Figure 21.

Place one humidity indicator card by each succulent plant (cactus) and one by each leafy plant (coleus). Cover the plants and the cards with clear plastic bags. Seal each bag with tape around the stem of the plant. Place the plants in the sun.

8. Subtract the dry weights from the wet weights. The difference is the weight of water that was in the leaves or the piece of succulent. (Since the weight of the foil did not change, the only difference is the water change.) To find the percentage of water in the leaves, divide the weight of water lost by the wet weight of the leaves and multiply by 100. Do the same for the succulent. Why are the percentages different?

9. Compare the ability of different plant leaves and stems to retain or store water. Why does a succulent (a plant with thick, waxy leaves) need to store more water than other types of plants? (**Hint:** *Think about the rainfall in a desert.*)

## Table 4.

## Humidity Index of Coleus (Leafy) and Cactus (Succulent) Over Time

| | Hour: | 0 | 1 | 2 | 3 | 4 | 5 | 6 | 7 | 8 |
|---|---|---|---|---|---|---|---|---|---|---|
| Coleus 1 | | | | | | | | | | |
| Coleus 2 | | | | | | | | | | |
| Average: | | | | | | | | | | |
| Cactus 1 | | | | | | | | | | |
| Cactus 2 | | | | | | | | | | |
| Average: | | | | | | | | | | |

# Results and Conclusions

Land plants have evolved many different ways of keeping, or conserving, the water they absorb. Plants have openings in their leaves called stomata that allow for the exchange of gases and water. Since much water is lost through the stomata, plants close their stomata when the water supply is low.

Some plants, such as cacti, have stems with a protective waxy coat. Other plants, such as the ocotillo shrub and the acacia tree, actually shed their leaves in times of drought to conserve water. The surface of plant leaves also can reduce water loss: Some plants have hairlike or fuzzy surfaces, some are shiny and reflect light, and others are very small to reduce surface area exposed to the sun. And some plants, called succulents, are able to store large quantities of water in their cells.

 Science Project Ideas

- Design an experiment to compare different plants' root tolerances for water in the soil. Use a desert plant and a wetland plant. Look at a cross section of a stem of a wetland plant. Notice that some have a spongy center so that gases can be transported to the roots.

- What could you do to a wet cloth or a saturated sponge placed in the sun to prevent water loss (to prevent it from drying out)? Hint: *Experiment with different coverings and shading arrangements. Find different leaves that show different adaptations for water conservation in plants.*

# EXPERIMENT 4.3

## Insulation and Heat Loss

### Question:
Does insulation slow the loss of heat?

### Hypothesis:
Insulation can slow heat loss.

### Materials:
- **an adult**
- 2 candy thermometers
- 4 widemouthed heat-resistant jars (see note)
- 2 shoeboxes
- insulating material (feathers or fake fur from a craft store, sawdust, Styrofoam pellets, foam)
- permanent marker
- stove
- pot
- oven mitts
- spoon
- can of lard (from the grocery store)
- glue or tape
- feathers
- water
- clock

Note: Each test group needs at least 2 jars. The more jars you include in the experiment, the more reliable your results will be.

Figure 22.

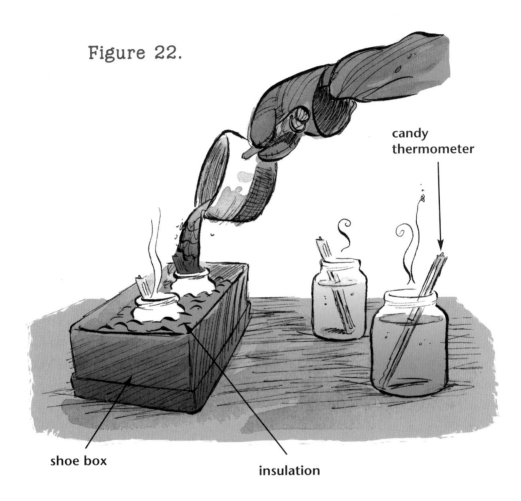

candy
thermometer

shoe box

insulation

What effect does insulation have on heat loss?

# Procedure:

1. Fill two shoeboxes with one type of insulating material (Styrofoam pellets, foam, sawdust, fake fur material, or feathers) and label them as A-1 and A-2. Make sure the insulating material reaches the neck of the jars. Now label two widemouthed, heat-resistant jars as B-1 and B-2 (see Figure 22). Place the jars in the shoeboxes.

2. **Have an adult** boil some water and, wearing oven mitts, fill each of the four jars with the water.

3. Record the temperature with a candy thermometer in each jar every 2 minutes for the next 20 minutes (move one thermometer between the two jars in each set). Then record the temperatures after 30 and 40 minutes. Graph the data (see Figure 23). Which set of jars cooled faster?

4. Take a can of lard (animal fat) and use a spoon to scoop out a place to put a jar of warm water. Compare the cooling rate of the insulated jar to a jar of warm water with no insulation.

5. Glue or tape layers of feathers to the outside of a jar of warm water. Does the length of time the water stays warm increase? What would limit the amount of fat (blubber), feathers, or fur an animal could have? (**Hint:** *Think about how many coats you could wear, or how fat you could be, and still be able to move around easily.*) What animals can survive the coldest weather? What adaptations allow them to survive there?

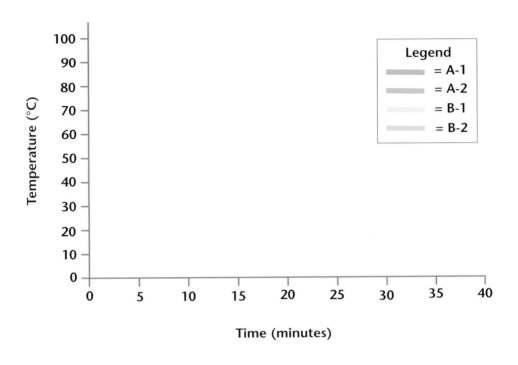

## Effect of Insulation on Cooling

**Figure 23.**

You can graph the results of the effect of insulation on the rate of cooling.

# Results and Conclusions

Think about what you do when it is cold. You may put on a sweater or a coat to insulate yourself. Insulation is one of the strategies that both mammals and birds, which are warm-blooded, have evolved to conserve body heat. Mammals and birds insulate themselves in different ways. Many mammals, such as horses and dogs, can grow thick hair or fur to keep warm. Other mammals, such as seals, whales, and dolphins, do not need wooly coats because they have thick layers of blubber under their skin to conserve body heat. And some mammals, such as polar bears, have both thick fur and thick layers of blubber.

Birds are covered with feathers. Fluffing the feathers traps air and provides an additional insulating layer. Oils spread over the feathers can provide a waterproof layer that is also insulating. And some birds, such as penguins, use each other for insulation—they huddle together to trap their body heat. But even penguins in Antarctica can get too hot. Since they cannot take off their coats, they stand with their wings out to let some body heat escape, or they jump into the cold water to cool off!

Science Project Idea

- Design some experiments to investigate the rate of heat loss with regard to size. Would a small jar of hot water cool faster than a large jar of hot water? Why can a large-bodied reptile, such as a crocodile, stay in the water longer than a smaller reptile? What are the advantages of this? Why would a small mammal need to eat more often than a large reptile?

# EXPERIMENT 4.4

## Leaves and Temperature Extremes

### Question:

Are some leaves adapted to withstand
temperature extremes?

### Hypothesis:

Some leaves are adapted to a variety of climates.

### Materials:

- **an adult**
- 2 succulent plants
  (aloe, jade, or
  Christmas cactus:
  see note)
- 2 house plants
  (fern, spider plant)
- measuring cup
- magnifying glass
- scale
- oven
- oven mitts
- aluminum foil
- evergreen needles
  (pine, hemlock,
  spruce, or fir trees)
- fresh green
  deciduous leaves
  (oak or maple trees)
- freezer
- newspaper
- water
- heavy books

*Note: Using most cactus plants is not recommended, as they are painful to handle!
A Christmas cactus is not a spiny cactus, so it is suitable for this experiment.*

## Procedure:

1. Use two plants with succulent leaves (thick, waxy leaves), such as a jade or an aloe plant. Use two other plants with leaves with no waxy covering or visible hair, such as a fern or a spider plant. Add ½ cup of water to each plant and wait at least four hours to make sure the plants have absorbed the water. Then take one leaf from each plant and examine each with a magnifying glass. What are the differences (leaf thickness, coating, etc.)?

2. Record the weight of six leaves from each of the four plants. This is the wet weight.

3. **Have an adult** place the leaves on a piece of aluminum foil and, using oven mitts, bake them in an oven at 250°F (121°C) for about an hour or until the leaves are crumbly. Reweigh them. This is the dry weight.

4. Subtract the dry weight from the wet weight. The difference is the weight of water that was in the leaves. (Since the weight of the foil did not change, the only difference is the water change.) To find the percentage of water in the leaves, divide the weight of the water lost by the wet weight and multiply by 100. Why are the percentages different?

5. Do not water the plants for several days. Observe the plants until one begins to wilt. Record the number of days that have passed.

   Why does one type of plant wilt and turn brown, and the other remain unchanged? How long does it take for the succulent plants to begin to wilt or to shrivel? How does water content in the leaves and leaf covering affect the ability of leaves to withstand heat?

6. Take some freshly picked needles from an evergreen tree (pine, hemlock, spruce, or fir) and some freshly picked leaves from a deciduous tree (a tree that loses its leaves in winter, such as a maple or an oak), or a houseplant without waxy leaves. Examine each leaf or needle with a magnifying glass. Record your observations.

7. Determine the water content of several leaves and needles. Place other needles and leaves in the freezer overnight. Record your observations. Compare the leaves' water content and covering. Which leaves are unchanged by freezing temperatures?

8. Present your data in a chart, including examples of the leaf types. You can press leaves without waxy coatings by placing them between pages of newspaper under a stack of heavy books for about two weeks. The longer you press them, the longer they will last.

# Results and Conclusions

You will not find pansies growing in the desert or cacti growing in Antarctica. This, very simply, is because plants have evolved to live in specific places within a certain range of conditions. These environmental conditions include the availability of water and nutrients and the temperature of the area. Temperature has a direct effect on the amount of water in a plant.

Hot temperatures can cause the plant to lose so much water that its cells shrivel and the plant dies. That is why many desert plants are succulents, meaning that their large, fleshy, waxy leaves can store a lot of water. The stored water is then available to the plant during times of drought.

Cold temperatures can cause water in a plant to freeze. Water expands when it freezes, which actually ruptures the plant cells, killing the plant. This is one reason that deciduous trees, such as oaks and maples, do not keep their leaves in the winter. Evergreen trees, such as pine and spruce, on the other hand, are adapted to keep their leaves (needles) all year. The needles have a thick, waxy coating that conserves the small amount of water the tree has and prevents the leaves (needles) from freezing.

# EXPERIMENT 4.5

## Bird Territory

### Question:

How do birds mark their territories and attract mates?

### Hypothesis:

Birds use certain behaviors to mark their territories and attract mates.

### Materials:

- outdoor area where you can watch birds in the spring
- bird field guides (check the library)
- watch
- paper
- pencil
- binoculars (optional)

# Procedure:

1. You need to gather data in spring. Choose an area in which you have observed bird activity: a meadow, a park, or a forest. Make a general map of the area, noting fields, trees, wetlands, and buildings.

2. For four days, record the bird activity for 30 to 45 minutes in the early morning. Mark the route(s) of the birds. Note what the bird is doing: carrying nesting material (twigs, mud, grasses), making vocalizations (songs or warning calls) or sounds (woodpecker's tap on a tree), looking for food, feeding a mate, or chasing other birds away. Are the birds singing mainly from certain spots? Why?

3. Use a bird field guide (and binoculars, if you can) to identify the birds. Can you also identify their songs using the field guide? Do both the male and female sing? Do many of same species of birds appear to be in the same area? Why do you think this is?

4. Make observations at different times of the day (at noon and early evening). Note the weather conditions. Does cloud cover or wind affect bird activity? If you are able to observe this same area in another season, notice if you see the same marking of the territories by singing and chasing out intruders. In the late summer, most birds have already nested—how much birdsong do you hear? In the fall and winter, what is the level of bird activity?

# Results and Conclusions

To reproduce, many animals, including birds, have to attract a mate and defend a territory. A territory is an area in which an animal builds a home and collects food. Since an area has only a certain amount of available food, animals have to defend the area they choose.

In some species of birds, the male will find a mate first, and then he will defend a territory. In other species, the male birds will build a nest (or nests) first, then the female chooses the nest she likes. For some birds, it seems that the male attracts a mate and marks his territory at the same time.

Each species attracts a mate and marks the territory in its own way, but the idea is to get noticed by a possible mate or to chase away an intruder. Birds do this by making noise. Many bird species, including songbirds and thrushes, sit at the tops of trees singing loudly in the spring. Some, such as the ruffed grouse, drum their feathers to make noise. Others, such as the woodpeckers, rap wood with their bills. If the male is not having success marking the territory by singing, he may display his feathers in a colorful flash to let others know he is there. And sometimes the bird will simply make warning calls or begin attacking the intruder. Birds usually defend their territories against other birds of the same species. For example, robins will chase away other robins.

The size of the territory depends on the type of birds. Small birds usually defend small territories. A robin's territory may be about a quarter of an acre or about 0.0004 square miles (0.001 km sq). Larger birds have larger territories—eagles may defend home territories that are dozens of square miles. Some birds, such as cliff swallows, live together in colonies.

Science Project Idea

- Some mammals also exhibit nesting behavior. If you keep gerbils, try filling their tank with a deep layer of soil. (If you use soil from outside, you won't have to clean the tank, since it is a system with microorganisms that will recycle the waste.) How long does it take the gerbils to dig a series of tunnels in the soil? Place pieces of newspaper in one corner and observe what happens. This is all part of nesting behavior. Will they use whatever paper you put in? Why or why not?

# EXPERIMENT 4.6

## Seed Dispersal and Wind

### Question:

How are some plants able to disperse seeds by wind?

### Hypothesis:

Some plants have adaptations for seed dispersal by wind. Other seeds can float or stick to an animal's fur.

### Materials:

- **an adult**
- seeds with wings (maple, dandelion, milkweed, aspen, grasses)
- tape measure
- seeds with no wings (beans, corn, sunflower, coconut, acorn, nuts)
- seeds from fruit (cranberry, apple, orange)
- fan
- stream
- dog, cat, piece of felt or fake fur and safety pin
- glue
- paper

# Procedure:

1. Collect at least two samples from the seed-with-wings group (maple, dandelion, milkweed, aspen, grasses) and seeds-without-wings group (beans, corn, sunflower, coconut, acorn, nuts). Glue a sample (except perhaps the coconut) of each seed to a chart. Examine the seeds and predict which you think would travel by wind.

2. Either inside or outside, put a fan on low and drop one of each seed from above the fan. Record what the seed does and measure out to where it finally lands. Why did certain seeds travel farther than others in the wind? How do those seeds differ from the others? By what other means could those seeds travel?

3. **With an adult**, find a stream in which to float seeds: use a cranberry, a coconut, an acorn, and grasses. Compare the travel distance. Would the amount of time a seed could remain in water and still be viable (able to live) be a factor in its reproductive success? Could you test this in fresh and in salt water?

4. Using your dog, cat, or a piece of fake fur (or felt) pinned to your pant leg, see how many seeds will stick to the fur. Take a walk to see how far the seeds can travel before they fall off. What other methods of seed dispersal can you observe? Is there a relationship between the plant's habitat and its method of seed dispersal?

# Results and Conclusions

Many seeds travel to places far from the parent plant. The benefit of seeds spreading, or seed dispersal, is that it increases the plant species' chances of survival. If all the seeds dropped right next to the parent plant, there might not be enough food, light, and water for them to grow. In addition, if growing conditions changed in that spot (perhaps from a flood or a drought), none of the plants would survive.

Seeds, like plants, come in many sizes. Seeds can be small, like a tomato seed, or quite large, like a coconut. It is not surprising, then, that seeds travel in many ways. Wind, water, and animals can all scatter seeds. Some seeds, such as dandelion seeds, are fluffy and fly easily in the wind. Some heavier seeds spin like helicopters—such as maple seeds, also called maple wings or samaras. Some seeds, such as coconuts and cranberries, can float in water. Some, such as acorns and nuts, are buried in different places by animals for later use, then forgotten. Other fleshy seeds (fruits) are eaten by animals and later excreted in a new location.

# EXPERIMENT 4.7

## Spines for Seed Protection

### Question:

How are seeds protected from being eaten by animals?

### Hypothesis:

Protective spines reduce the number of seeds eaten by animals.

### Materials:

- 4 people
- large marshmallows
- watch with a second hand
- toothpicks
- mittens or masking tape

### Procedure:

1. For each participant, follow this procedure: Insert 20 toothpicks into one marshmallow, 10 into another, 5 into another, and leave another without any toothpicks.

2. Have the person either put his hands in mittens without using the thumb or wrap some masking tape around his hand so that the thumbs and fingers are all together (most animals do not have opposable thumbs).

3. For each of the marshmallow/toothpick combinations, record the time it takes each person to remove the "spines" and get to the food at the center. Which spine arrangement afforded the most protection (took the longest to eat)? It takes energy for a plant to grow spines that protect the seeds. Does it seem to be an effective strategy? Draw your conclusions. Did you prove or disprove the hypothesis?

4. Does the length of the spines make a difference? Do you think animals would try to eat the spiniest marshmallows if there were plenty of spineless ones to be found? Design an experiment with your friends. Present the variety of marshmallows and give them a fixed amount of time to eat as many as possible.

## Results and Conclusions

If you don't want to get eaten by something, you can hide, fight, or just taste so bad (or be so poisonous) that your enemy learns not to eat those like you. It makes sense that both plants and animals use these strategies for protection. Some plants have spines, thorns, and bad taste or poisons. Others have tough bark or seed coatings. Some animals also have spines (porcupines), claws (cats), poisons (cobras), and hard coats (armadillo).

# Glossary

**adaptation**—A characteristic of an organism that has developed to allow it to live in a particular place; the change that was made to acquire that characteristic.

**behavior**—Any response to a stimuli; it can have a genetic base (instinct), or it can be learned.

**biodiversity**—A term that became popular in the 1990s, it, describes the diversity of life (or number of different types of species) in an area.

**biology**—The study of living organisms; the life processes of an organism.

**botany**—The study of plants.

**cell**—The smallest unit of life that can survive and reproduce on its own. The simplest cell contains a membrane that surrounds water containing organic molecules and DNA.

**cuticle**—The waxy or fatty covering on the exposed cells of many land plants. It decreases the water lost through evaporation.

**DNA (deoxyribonucleic acid)**—A molecule containing all the genetic information of an organism; consists of two strands of twisted nucleotides in a sequence that encodes the instructions for making proteins.

**genes**—Units of DNA on a chromosome that contain all the information to give an organism its particular traits.

**habitat**—The place in which an organism or a species usually lives.

**metabolism**—All the chemical reactions within a cell that allow the cell to acquire and to use energy for growth, survival, and reproduction.

**nutrient**—A substance from the environment necessary for the survival, growth, and reproduction of an organism.

**phloem**—Tissue that transports concentrated sugar solution throughout the plant.

**photosynthesis**—The series of chemical reactions in a plant powered by light energy in which low-energy inorganic molecules (water and carbon dioxide) are combined to make sugars.

**phototropism**—A reaction to light.

**pollen**—Sperm-bearing male cells in plants.

**predator**—An organism that hunts and eats other organisms.

**prey**—An organism hunted and eaten by other organisms.

**stomata**—The openings on a leaf or stem that open and close to regulate the exchange of gases and water with the environment.

**territory**—An area of land defended against competitors by an animal to meet its needs for growth, survival, and reproduction.

**xylem**—Tissue that conducts water and minerals throughout the plant.

# Appendix

# SCIENCE SUPPLY COMPANIES

**Carolina Biological Supply Company**
2700 York Road
Burlington, NC 27215-3398
(800) 334-5551
http://www.carolina.com

**Connecticut Valley Biological**
**Supply Company**
82 Valley Road
P.O. Box 326
Southampton, MA 01073
(800) 628-7748
http://www.ctvalleybio.com

**Delta Education**
80 Northwest Boulevard
P.O. Box 3000
Nashua, NH 03061-3000
(800) 258-1302
http://www.delta-education.com

**Edmund Scientifics**
60 Pearce Avenue
Tonawanda, NY 14150-6711
(800) 728-6999
http://scientificsonline.com

**Educational Innovations, Inc.**
362 Main Avenue
Norwalk, CT 06851
(888) 912-7474
http://www.teachersource.com

**Fisher Science Education**
4500 Turnberry Drive
Hanover Park, IL 60133
(800) 955-1177
http://www.fisheredu.com

**Frey Scientific**
80 Northwest Boulevard
Nashua, NH 03063
(800) 225-3739
http://www.freyscientific.com/

**NASCO-Fort Atkinson**
901 Janesville Avenue
P.O. Box 901
Fort Atkinson, WI 53538-0901
(800) 558-9595
http://www.nascofa.com/

**NASCO-Modesto**
4825 Stoddard Road
P.O. Box 3837
Modesto, CA 95352-3837
(800) 558-9595
http://www.enasco.com

**Sargent-Welch**
P.O. Box 4130
Buffalo, NY 14217
(800) 727-4368
http://www.sargentwelch.com

**Science Kit & Boreal Laboratories**
777 East Park Drive
P.O. Box 5003
Tonawanda, NY 14151-5003
(800) 828-7777
http://sciencekit.com

**Ward's Natural Science**
P.O. Box 92912
Rochester, NY 14692-9012
(800) 962-2660
http://www.wardsci.com

# Further Reading

Bochinski, Julianne Blair. *The Complete Workbook for Science Fair Projects*. Hoboken, N.J.: Wiley, 2005.

Juettner, Bonnie. *Photosynthesis*. Detroit: KidHaven Press, 2005.

Llewellyn, Claire. *Plants of the World*. North Mankato, Minn.: Smart Apple Media, 2007.

Vecchione, Glen. *Blue Ribbon Science Projects*. New York: Sterling Publishing Company, 2005.

Walker, Denise. *Adaptation and Survival*. North Mankato, Minn.: Smart Apple Media, 2006.

Yablonski, Judy. *Plant and Animal Cells: Understanding the Differences Between Plant and Animal Cells*. New York: Rosen Publishing Group, 2005.

# Internet Addresses

National Geographic Kids. "Creature Features."
    <http://kids.nationalgeographic.com/Animals/CreatureFeature/>

Rader's Biology4Kids.com. "Plants."
    <http://www.biology4kids.com/files/plants_main.html/>

TryScience. "Experiments."
    <http://www.tryscience.org/experiments/experiments_home.html/>

# Index